Juan Benet

Twayne's World Authors Series

Janet Pérez, Editor of Spanish Literature

Texas Tech University

TWAS 685

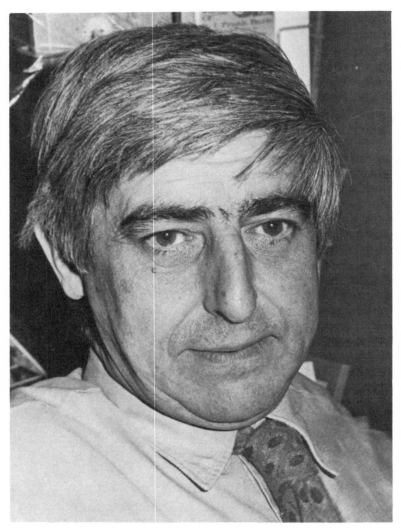

JUAN BENET
Photograph by Santacana Jr.

Juan Benet

By Vicente Cabrera

Colorado State University

Twayne Publishers • *Boston*

Juan Benet

Vicente Cabrera

Copyright © 1983 by G. K. Hall & Company
All Rights Reserved
Published by Twayne Publishers
A Division of G. K. Hall & Company
70 Lincoln Street
Boston, Massachusetts 02111

Book Production by Marne B. Sultz
Book Design by Barbara Anderson

Printed on permanent/durable acid-free
paper and bound in the United States of
America.

Library of Congress Cataloging in Publication Data

Cabrera, Vicente.
  Juan Benet.

  (Twayne's world authors series ; TWAS 685)
  Bibliography: p. 146
  Includes index.
  1. Benet, Juan—Criticism and interpretation.
I. Title. II. Series.
PQ6652.E5Z57 1983   863'.64   82–21213
ISBN 0–8057–6532–8

To
Lisa and Jay

Contents

About the Author

Vicente Cabrera, born in Ecuador, received the M.A. and Ph.D. in Spanish from the University of Massachusetts at Amherst in 1970 and 1972, respectively. Presently, he is Professor of the Department of Foreign Languages and Literatures at Colorado State University. He is cofounder and coeditor of the *Journal of Spanish Studies: Twentieth Century* and has published four books containing essays on Aleixandre, Asturias, Cela, Delibes, García Márquez, J. Guillén, Hernández, and Salinas. His numerous articles have appeared in many journals in the United States, Mexico, Puerto Rico, and Spain.

Preface

The purpose of this book is to introduce to the English-speaking reader the life and works of the Spanish novelist Juan Benet, one of the most important, controversial, and influential novelists of the Spanish language today. His unique, complex, and ever-growing literary output includes fifteen short stories, six novelettes, five novels, two fables, three plays, and six books of essays. Even though literary criticism on his works is already extensive and Malcolm A. Compitello's excellent compilation attests to this, it still remains uneven, inasmuch as only a few of his novels are repeatedly studied. The most comprehensive critique written so far on the author is David Herzberger's *The Novelistic World of Juan Benet,* which discusses his literary theory and five novels, one of them being *Una tumba* [A Tomb], which I include among the novelettes. To my knowledge no study has been written on his literary production as a whole. The present book responds to this need. I have organized the material according to genres, and the works within a genre are arranged chronologically. Since none of Benet's works has been translated into English, although some are currently being translated, all translations from the original Spanish are mine.

I would like to express my deep gratitude to Professor Janet Pérez from Texas Tech University and William Moseley from Colorado State University for their careful reading of the manuscript and their valuable suggestions; to Juan Benet for providing me with recent information that I could not have found elsewhere and for the authorization allowing me to quote from his works; to Barbara Probost Solomon for the invaluable information on Juan Benet given to me through our conversations and skillfully developed in her nonfiction-fictional periplus, *Arriving Where We Started;* and, to George MacMurray, who brought me from Spain in 1973 the first book by Juan Benet.

Vicente Cabrera

Colorado State University

Chronology

1927   Juan Benet born in Madrid on 7 October.

1936   The Civil War broke out. His father was shot.

1938   Moved with his family to San Sebastián.

1939   Returned to Madrid for his high-school studies.

1944   Completed his *bachillerato* (high-school degree).

1948   Enrolled in the School of Engineering.

1954   Received degree in Engineering.

1956   Married Nuria Jordana and moved to the Spanish province of León to work in his new career.

1959   Moved to Oviedo and wrote *Nunca llegarás a nada* [You Will Never Get Anywhere].

1961   Published *You Will Never Get Anywhere* at his own expense.

1962   For professional reasons moved to Vegamián (León) and began writing *Volverás a Región* [You Will Return to Región].

1965   *La inspiración y el estilo* [Inspiration and Style], his first book of essays.

1966   His brother Francisco died in a car accident in Iran.

1968   *You Will Return to Región.*

1969   Received the *Biblioteca Breve* Literary Prize for *Una meditación* [A Meditation].

1970   *Una tumba* [A Tomb] and *Puerta de tierra* [Door of Dust].

1971   *Teatro* [Theater], a three-play collection.

1972   *Un viaje de invierno* [A Winter Journey]; received the *Nueva Crítica* Literary Award.

1973   *5 narraciones y 2 fábulas* [5 Narrations and 2 Fables] and *Sub rosa,* a collection of short stories.

1974   *La otra casa de Mazón* [The Mazón's Other House]. His wife died.

1976   *El ángel del señor abandona a Tobías* [The Angel of the Lord Abandons Tobit] and *En ciernes* [In Blossom].

1977   *Cuentos completos* [Complete Short Stories], *¿Qué fue la Guerra Civil?* [What was the Civil War?], and *En el estado* [In the State].

1978   *Del pozo y del Numa* [Of the Well and of Numa].

Chapter One

The Birth of a Novelist:
"My Mother Is a fish"

Juan Benet was born in Madrid on 7 October 1927. A Catalan from his father's side, a Basque from his mother's, and a Castilian by birth, Benet has spent most of his life in the Spanish capital. He began to experience the horrors of the Spanish Civil War (1936–1939) at the age of nine, when his father, Tomás Benet, for reasons unknown, was killed by a firing squad. This may explain why this war is a major recurrent image in his fiction. It is usually assimilated into a given work as echoes or sensations of an innocuous past upon which the emptiness of the present must rest. Having lost their father, the family (his mother, Teresa Goitia, his older brother Francisco, and his sister Marisol) moved to the Basque city of San Sebastián, remaining there until the war was over. They returned to Madrid in 1939 for Juan's *bachillerato* (high-school studies), which he completed in 1944. From his religious high school, Benet learned one thing: to dislike what they taught him. There he acquired the desire to develop a taste which would run contrary to that of his mentors, the same mentors who regarded Pemán's and Gabriel y Galán's poems as "sublime and exquisite," or Pereda and Father Coloma as the masters of the Spanish novel.[1] Between 1944, when he finished high school, and 1948, when he enrolled in the School of Engineering, something quite crucial occurred in his literary formation: the discovery and subsequent exploration of William Faulkner's fictional world. The discovery took place in the spring of 1945, when, looking for a given book at a used bookstore, on San Bernardo Street in Madrid, he accidentally knocked down another which fell open onto the floor, showing on its left page the following:

> "Vardaman:
> My mother is a fish"[2]

Suddenly, the poetic, surreal, enigmatic nature of the line had
sparked Benet's curiosity for the master's fabulous fiction, most of
which he read between then and the summer of 1967, when he
temporarily put it aside.[3] Faulkner's decisive influence has been
repeatedly acknowledged by Benet himself. Also he read at this time
Proust, Joyce, Melville, Sartre, Malraux, and Camus. And to obtain
books which were not allowed in Spain, he established a secret
connection between Paris and Madrid: at the other end of the smug-
gling line was his brother Francisco (Paco), who was studying at
the Sorbonne with a scholarship from the French government.[4] On
his return from Paris, where he went to visit his brother toward the
end of 1949, he was momentarily and mistakenly arrested at the
border (Hendaya) by the Spanish police. The reason: they confused
him with his brother Paco, who with the assistance of two American
girls (Barbara Probost Solomon and Barbara Mailer, Norman Mailer's sister) had helped two Republican prisoners (Nicolás Sánchez
Albornoz and Manolo Lamana) escape from Cuelgamuros. The following is Benet's letter relating the incident to his brother.

They asked me if I was Benet y Goitia. I replied: "Of course, sure I am.
What would you like to know?" Did you know Manolo Lamana and Nicolás
Sánchez Albornoz? "Oh, yes. They are great kids. Very good friends of
mine." Then they told me that I was under arrest. I let them talk all they
wanted to, until I realized that they knew all the details of the escape
from Cuelgamuros . . . and that they wanted to catch Benet y Goitia,
whom they accuse of everything imaginable. Then I told them: "Oh, for
sure you are referring to my brother Francisco. He is alive and in Paris,
having a good time. I just spent a week with him. Things are going
smoothly for him in Paris." Paquito, they were enraged. I don't know
why. I was very polite. I thanked them for chatting with me. Very rude,
those Spanish police. Paco, you are a wanted fugitive. Don't come near
Spain. Love, Juan

This is also the time when he managed to bring into Spain, in his
backpack, a few more books by Faulkner.[5] As mentioned before, in
1948 he enrolled in the School of Engineering and received his
degree in 1954. By then, he had already published in *Revista Española*
(1953) an amateurish, traditional play, *Max,* and had also written
a novel, *El Guarda* [The Guard], which for lack of an adventurous
publisher never appeared. One infers from Benet's history on his
first published novel that *The Guard* (the title is an allusion to the

famous Numa of his later fiction) was indeed the thematic and stylistic anticipation of *Volverás a Región* [You Will Return to Región].[6] In 1956, just married and with his new degree in engineering, he moved to León and Oviedo to build dams and bridges as well as to construct his own mythical world of Región, where, with the exception of his novel, *En el estado* [In The State], all his major fiction takes place. In these northwestern provinces, he wrote three books: (1) *Nunca llegarás a nada* [You Will Never Get Anywhere], a collection of four novelettes which he published in 1961 at his own expense and with the assistance of his friend Vicente Giner, a publisher who, from the beginning, was skeptical about the book's marketability because it was "too difficult to read";[7] (2) his first book of essays, *La inspiración y el estilo* [Inspiration and Style], wherein he laid the foundations of his literary theory and the principles of his ongoing fiction; and (3) *You Will Return to Región,* for whose "lack of dialogues" its author again encountered problems with publishers who demanded easier, more readable novels. But this time, Benet met with better luck; in 1967 Destino Publishing Company from Barcelona accepted the manuscript for publication. It appeared the same year and, with the exception of one or two reviews, the new book, just as had *You Will Never Get Anywhere,* passed basically unnoticed by critics and public alike. The next year, however, Benet's anonymity ended when he was awarded the coveted *Biblioteca Breve* Literary Prize for *Una meditación* [A Meditation], which catapulted its author to fame. Only then people realized that Juan Benet had already published two other works which were equally as unique as the prize-winning novel. Ever since, his prestige and fame at home and abroad have consistently increased with the high quality of his new literary output published in the 1970s: four novels, fifteen short stories, two novelettes, three plays, and five books of essays. His distinctively unique, complex fictional world, his forceful, innovative style, and his very controversial ideas have made Juan Benet the leading "new" novelist in Spain today.

Chapter Two
A Novelist
without a Generation

In order to determine Benet's place among contemporary Spanish novelists, as well as to weigh and qualify his overall importance among them, it is necessary to review the contemporary Spanish novel's evolution between 1940 and 1967, that is, between the time peace was restored in the country and the year when Benet's first major work was published. It is agreed among literary critics and historians that the Spanish novel of the 1940s differs from that of the 1950s, just as much as the latter differs from the novel written in the 1960s, a three-part distinction which Gonzalo Sobejano establishes in order to classify the post–Civil War Spanish novel into *Novela existencial* ("Existential Novel"), *Novela social* ("Social Novel"), and *Novela estructural* ("Structural Novel"), obviously a useful classification whose accuracy and clarity contrasts with many others that, rather than helping, further confuse the issue.[1] This is the case of Eugenio de Nora's, Juan Ignacio Ferreras's and Antonio Iglesias Laguna's unnecessary and pedantic divisions and subdivisions of the novel's evolution.[2] It also seems that the generation method is not quite useful in this case since there are many writers who, like Camilo J. Cela, Miguel Delibes, and Juan Goytisolo, have throughout the years changed stylistically and therefore abandoned the basic literary patterns for which their generation became famous. In view of this, I have chosen to base this review on the chronological succession of those works which stand out in the development of the genre.

The Novel of the 1940s:
Tremendism and Existentialism

With few exceptions, very little of importance appeared in the first decade following the Spanish Civil War. Many factors contributed to this sterility: (1) the forced or self-imposed exile many

4

writers had to undergo to avoid persecution or find a freer environment where they could continue with their literary creation; (2) the cultural and, in this case, novelistic vacuum resulting from the departure of those writers and the new government's policy of censorship vigorously implemented to eliminate any work that did not conform with the spirit of the regime; (3) the problem of how to restore the continuity of the novel, which was broken between 1936 and 1939. By following the line of Valle-Inclán's aesthetic prose, of Unamuno's philosophical novel, of Pío Baroja's stark realism, of Benito Pérez Galdós's more classical and traditional realism? Or by finding a new formula that would satisfy the individual author trapped in a culturally and morally devastated society? The impasse was broken, and indeed quite successfully, when, in 1942, Camiló José Cela published his first novel: *La familia de Pascual Duarte* [Pascual Duarte's Family], a deceivingly simple confession of a man (Pascual) who strives to convince the reader that he is in no way responsible for his criminal behavior (he killed in cold blood three people, one of them his mother, and two animals), that he had no choice since destiny and/or the special social circumstances in which he had lived made him what he was. To convince the reader of his innocence, he skillfully manipulates a system of reasoning that seems to be logical but which, in reality, is nonsensical since often what he says does not conform with what he does, an ironic perspective that runs throughout the entire novel.[3] A truculent, ambitious, and ironic work such as this, appearing in the Spanish novelistic vacuum left by the war, obviously attracted immediate public attention and brought to its young author instant success and fame. Hopes were high. The Spanish novel was reborn. And *tremendismo* (a type of realism characterized by the emphasis on horror and violence) was coined as a label to identify those works following *Pascual Duarte's Family*.

The second and last surprise of the decade came in 1945 when a young, unknown writer, Carmen Laforet, published her first and (so far) her only good novel: *Nada* [Nothing], another existential and somewhat *tremendista* work concerning a young woman, Andrea, who recounts her experience when, hoping to find a new, more exciting life and an appropriate environment for her self-realization, she goes to live at her relative's home in Barcelona. A few days have passed when she begins to realize that neither life nor the place are as she thought they would be. Instead, she learns that both are hells of despair and nothingness. Irony is again the main structuring element of the work; from the *nada* ("emptiness") surrounding her, she learns ultimately *something,* the *nada* of life itself.

In addition to the universal scope of these two novels resulting from the crude confrontation of man with his world, the authors' criticism of Spanish society is also evident. This was a society whose wounds from a fratricidal war were still open, and whose psychological and moral deterioration the authors tried to portray via an ironic, sordid, and violent realism. Realism became the prevalent formula to restore the continuity of the novel broken by the Civil War. Cela indicated in 1944 that the novel should be "the reflection of reality, of a beautiful or of a filthy reality."[4] And Juan Antonio de Zunzunegui made similar remarks to the effect that reality should be everything in art.[5] As a result, Baroja, the realist from the Generation of 1898, came to be their model, their last great master of the past.[6]

The Novel of the 1950s: Neo-Realism

Unlike the 1940s, the decade of the 1950s was a very productive period, if not for the quality of the works (few are the exceptions), then for the number of novels and the massive proliferation of novelists. As early as 1951 the Spanish novel took a new direction, toward a more transparent, direct, objective realism, committed to the improvement of postwar Spain. Again, the initiator of this new trend was Camilo J. Cela, whose *La colmena* [The Beehive, 1951] was published, for problems of censorship, not in Spain but in Argentina. With more than three hundred characters taken from all sectors of society and employing new structural techniques and a great deal of irony, humor, and cinematographic illusion, Cela masterfully portrayed the empty and nonsensical lives of those living in Madrid in the 1940s. They all appeared, as Cela explained, "immersed in their own insignificance," in their gray, quotidian, vulgar existence.[7] Unlike *Pascual Duarte's Family,* where the use of time, space, character, and structure was conventional, *The Beehive* represented in Spain an innovative, technical, artistic achievement and, in the author's career, a step forward that enhanced his prestige as a novelist both at home and abroad. As new writers appeared on the literary scene, Neo-Realism acquired the form of a very strong and coherent movement that would last well into the 1960s. Most of its members had experienced the Civil War in their childhood and began to write on their postwar society in the 1950s, hence the name with which they were identified: *La generación de medio siglo* ("The Mid-Century Generation"), a label coined by their contemporary and active spokesman, José María Castellet. The milestones of this generation are *Los bravos* (1954), by Jesús Fernández Santos; *Duelo en el Paraíso* (1955), by Juan Goytisolo; *El Jarama* (1956), by Rafael Sánchez Ferlosio; and *Nuevas amistades* (1959), by Juan García Hartelano. Other members belonging to this group but whose first works of social realism appeared in the 1960s are Juan Marsé, Alfonso Grosso, Antonio Ferres, and Armando López Salinas.

Basically, all Neo-Realist writers firmly believed in the novel's ethic and social function. They believed literature was a propitious instrument to transform society, to show the world the many injustices under which large groups of Spaniards live. As a result, factory, farm, city, and mine workers came to populate the novels of this period, as well as the bourgeoisie with its parasitic habits and boredom. As their mission was to reproduce and report all the social inadequacies as accurately and objectively as possible, novelistic imagination, artistic elaboration, and depth, if not totally discarded and condemned as symptoms of escapism and dishonesty, were at least rare. To ensure that the message reached the public, language was by and large stripped of vagueness, subtleties, and ambiguities. Linguistically, they deemed it necessary to reproduce the frivolous, trivial vulgarity of the characters' lives; to intensify the objectivity of the narrative, they assimilated in their works the linguistic peculiarities of the groups or regions they chose to portray.

In two international panel discussions on the novel, held in Formentor in 1959 and in Florence in 1962, the Italian and the Spanish novelists in attendance agreed on the social function of literature, against the French who, headed by Alain Robbe-Grillet, vehemently defended the artistic freedom of the writer and his exclusive commitment to the genre's development.[8] For more than ten years these Spanish novelists would enthusiastically maintain this *engagé* type of literature, a literature that with few exceptions degenerated into mediocre journalism.

The Novel of the 1960s: Subjectivism

Social realism took a different, more refined perspective in 1962 with the appearance of *Tiempo de Silencio* [Time of Silence], by Luis Martín Santos, who died in a car accident two years later. In *Time of Silence,* Martín Santos criticized the entire social fabric of Spanish society with a new, revolutionary, more elaborate language; his intention was not to repeat the same diction of the past, but to destroy it, and with its destruction to create a pattern of expression that would serve to embody his ironic and sarcastic view not only of Spain, its institutions, and sacred traditions, but also of modern man and his world. Both in language and content this novel represented a more ambitious experiment which would later be followed by some of the Neo-Realists of the 1950s as well as imitated by others from previous generations, as evidenced by the appearance of novels such as *Señas de identidad* and *Revindicación del Conde don Julián* (1966), by Juan Goytisolo; *Parábola del náufrago* (1969), by Miguel Delibes; and *San Camilo, 1936* (1969), by C.J. Cela. *Volverás a Región* and *Una meditación* are the first two major novels with which Juan Benet entered the literary arena. Unlike the realistic novel of the 1950s and 1940s, these works of *contraola* ("counterwave")[9] incorporate modern experimentations with point of view, character, time and space. With a more complex novelistic structure, levels of reality proliferate, intricate narrative discourses emerge, and the effects of the novel as a whole become greater. What were the factors contributing to this change in attitude, taste, and style on the part of these and other writers? Several: (1) Spain began to open itself up more and more to the world. Censorship became more tolerant. (2) Through an improved educational system the reading public grew in number and in literary awareness. (3) Foreign books became more available. (4) The new Latin American novel channeled through the editors of Seix Barral gained popularity within Spain, as did the French New Novel, the same *nouveau roman* whose founding father, Robbe-Grillet (at the two international conventions previously mentioned), was criticized by the very Spaniards who later accepted, at least in part, his precepts, advocating a free, *desengagé* novel. (5) The exhausting repetition of the same novelistic formula became intolerable. "Our young novelists," observed José Batllo in 1964, "have not managed to do anything but to keep on repeating the same formulae, hoping in vain they would be useful to them forever."[10] The abuse was such, comments Alvaro Cunqueiro, that "you opened a book and all were the same."[11]

From what has been produced in the 1970s it seems that the social novel of the 1950s is for all practical purposes extinct, and the novel of the *contraola* alive and dynamic, seeking more challenging and exciting formulae to enrich its structure, its narrative discourse, and its manipulation of time, character, space, and point of view. All this is evident in *Juan sin Tierra* (1975) and *Makbara* (1980), by Juan Goytisolo; *Eterna memoria* (1974), by Ramón Hernández; *Fragmentos de Apocalipsis* (1978), by Gonzalo Torrente Ballester; *Los verdes de mayo hasta el mar* (1976), by Luis Goytisolo; and Benet's intricate body of fiction which increased steadily in the 1970s.

Chronologically, Juan Benet belongs to the Mid-Century Generation; aesthetically, however, he does not. His ideas on literature and on the novel are the antithesis of the group's. He stated: ". . . when I try to write literature, I abide by literary principles which I have striven to extract and purify ever since I started, for the first time, to write a book. . . ."[12] Indeed Benet clearly showed from his earliest work, *You Will Never Get Anywhere* (1961), a distinctive preference for the novel as a work of art wherein style is of utmost importance. Since he did not share the group's novelistic precept that the writer's moral and civic commitment is to change society, logically he never took part in its literary activities. Perhaps the only time when he indirectly did so was when he published a somewhat "Neo-Realist" play, *Max,* in *Revista Española* (1953), a prominent literary journal closely identified with the group and whose content basically reflected its aesthetic preferences and inclinations.[13] Benet would like to forget this play; when he published the collection of his theater in 1971 he did not include it or even mention its existence. The gap between him and the group became more conspicuous when in December 1970 *Cuadernos para el diálogo* published three items: (1) Benet's "Reflexiones sobre Galdós" [Reflections on Galdós];[14] (2) what he and five other contemporary novelists (J. M. Caballero Bonald, José M. Guelbenzu, Carmen Martín Gaité, A. Martínez Menchén, and Isaac Montero, the moderator) had said at a panel discussion on topics dealing with the novel, its language, its function, etc.; and (3) Benet's letter "Respuesta al Señor Montero" [Answer to Mr. Montero] countering Montero's written attack on Benet not only for what he had said about social realism but also for the disruptive way in which he treated the discussion, turning the whole affair into a fiasco.[15]

In his "Reflexiones sobre Galdós" (an open letter sent by Benet to the editor of *Cuadernos para el diálogo* declining an invitation to write on Galdós for the journal) he vigorously condemns Galdós's novelistic world as lacking in linguistic elaboration, literary imagination, and craftsmanship. Benet regards Galdos's entire novelistic output not as an authentic, refined, fictional world for aesthetic enjoyment, but a sociohistorical compendium of nineteenth-century Spain, comparable to Zola's or Balzac's mediocrities written on nineteenth-century France. Benet is not the first to attack Galdós; there were others before him. The Nicaraguan poet Rubén Darío was one and, of course, Valle-Inclán, with his famous line, half-serious and half-humorous—*Don Benito el garbancero* ("Don Benito the garbanzo dealer")—was the other. Yet Benet's attack on one of the most popular, even "sacred" figures of Spanish realism reached unprecedented proportions when he called him a "national disaster," a second-rate writer who, for purely nationalistic reasons, had been elevated to the rank of a literary patriarch. [16] In the panel discussion and in his letter to Montero (another social realist writer) Benet maintained the same position he has always maintained throughout the years: that literature and sociology are two different entities, that to assign a social function to the novel is to undermine the potential of a work of art, and that Spanish social realism has unvaryingly been a vulgar type of literature ("as vulgar as a shoe and as aromatic as an insecticide"), written for a public that had no choice but to "tolerate and even applaud under the coercion of collective guilt. . . ."[17] With these polemical letters Benet did consolidate, once and for all, the image of a very controversial writer, to be admired by few and disliked by many, the former being mainly new avant-garde groups in Barcelona, and the latter, more conservative circles in Madrid.

Chapter Three

The Essay: Reflections, Theories, and Polemics

There are few Spanish contemporary novelists who, in the same degree as Benet, have devoted themselves both to literary creation and to literary theory and analytic thought. In addition to his numerous novelettes, novels, short stories, and plays, Benet has published six books of essays covering a variety of areas: literature, linguistics, music, politics, philosophy, education, etc. Those books, written in barely more than a decade, are *La inspiración y el estilo* [Inspiration and Style, 1965], *Puerta de tierra* [Door of Dust, 1970], *En ciernes* [In Blossom, 1976], *El ángel del Señor abandona a Tobías* [The Angel of the Lord Abandons Tobit, 1976], *¿Qué fué la Guerra Civil?* [What Was the Civil War?, 1976], and *Del pozo y del Numa* [Of the Well and of Numa, 1978], an impressive output for an engineer whose writing, he claims, is only a pastime.[1] Besides his vast knowledge and assiduous intellectual curiosity, most of the essays show Benet's sharp perception and subtle method of analysis, so subtle indeed that it requires from the reader a great deal of concentration and patience, particularly because the complexity of the analysis is conveyed through a flowing, rich, conceptual, metaphoric, and sometimes ironic language. In view of both the quality and the quantity of his critical production it is safe to say that Benet is one of the most important essayists in Spain today.

Literary Theory

From the essays published thus far one notices that by and large the most coherent and most complete body of thought is Benet's literary theory. And since this is the most useful tool to understand better his narrative production, most of this chapter will be devoted to its exposition and analysis.[2]

Inspiration and Style. The these two key concepts in literature become the main themes of Benet's first book of essays, *Inspiration and Style,* written long before his first major novel, *You Will Return to Región,* was published, meaning that the writer was fully cognizant of the intricacies and problems of the creative process. The cornerstone of his discussion is that inspiration (that *soplo divino,* "divine whisper," vision, or dispensation which the Greeks believed proceeded from the gods to special men) comes to "a writer only when he possesses a style" (*Inspiration,* 27–28). And the special *estado de gracia* ("state of grace") the writer needs to gain in order to receive the divine inspiration is furnished or provided *only* by style. Style allegedly creates that special state of grace whereby the author receives inspiration, enabling him both to enjoy a more direct and broader vision of life and to overcome his limited human condition. Therefore style is what ultimately makes the writer God-like, seeing what no one else can see and saying what no one else can say. This Benet calls the state of *endiosamiento,* of being like God (37–38). After explaining this conceptual mechanism, Benet cautiously attempts to define each component.

Inspiration is envisioned as perhaps a special gesture of the will, very distant from consciousness or reason (53). The question Benet must answer at this point is, specifically when or how inspiration "sprouts" (*brota*) once the style is already there? The answer: "when between the writer's two poles [will and consiousness] there is a certain state of tension created by the will, with some independence from consciousness. I do not say," continues Benet, "that it [inspiration] has necessarily to appear in a way unbeknown to knowledge, but only that it is or can be independent from it, a spark resulting from a tension to which it [consciousness] is alien even though it might be aware [of tension]" (53). The fact that reason "might be aware" of the tension causing the specific inspiration does not mean that it will control the whole creative process. No, because style is the ultimate force that takes it over, and style was the force that originally made possible such a tension. After the tension appears, style is to start dictating "the general image of the universe," with all its complexities and enigmas (108).

What is style? Benet realizes the difficulty in defining it. He says that "one can imagine that style is nothing but the result of some unique conditions—personality, character traits, sediments of education, the sublimation of a vocation or of a pastime—applied to the realization of a function" (157). More than a rigorous and complete definition, this is only a preliminary statement that serves Benet as a starting point in his exploration of the nature and mechanics of style. To what kind of "function" are those unique conditions applied? Benet answers: "Undoubtedly it will be to an intelligible function," accepted by the writer's fellow men (157). If such is the case, then that function must have to go through the same sieve that reason requires for all human inventions. But there is still another sieve, more strict and severe than the former, constituted by the norms regulating the specific "function" to be executed. The rules are, for instance, of harmony if the individual sings, of syntax if he writes, of logic if he thinks, etc. At this point two alternatives are left to the individual in order to execute a function with a personal and distinctive style: either his personality is subtle enough to sift through that last sieve or else he simply does not need to go through it because he is able to arrive at the end of the test without ever having to justify anything to anyone. The paradox obviously becomes more flagrant in the case of the writer who, by virtue of his personal style, has not only bypassed the test but also has allowed his reason to accept the sieve of norms which he (with his style) will openly defy and totally ignore. And until this moment, reason has been incapable of dominating or controlling or measuring the artist's personal style. From these considerations we conclude, affirms Benet, that style is not rational. It surpasses the light of reason to reach and delve into the darkest areas and capture their hidden sensations through images and visions that will fascinate the reader regardless of whether or not he understands them (157–58).

Style and Information. It is clear from the preceding discussion that for Benet the literary work can be of interest not for what it says, but for the way in which it is said, in other words, not for *el asunto* ("the subject") but for its style, because a work of art should be conceived as a purely technical problem, as a challenge which the writer accepts, hoping to succeed through his personal style (135). Benet is very critical of the *costumbrista* novel (depicting the regional manner and customs) and of the Naturalist and Realist novel of the nineteenth century and those so-called "Neo-Realist" Spanish novels of the twentieth century[3] because they are more informational than literary, that is, they respond more to nonliterary criteria, to sociological or scientific needs rather than to artistic and technical convictions. Zola's or Balzac's works are merely sociological monuments that now no one is interested in, except as mere curiosities of the past, because they were written without thinking of them as formal or stylistic achievements but simply as informational vehicles, as a means to inform readers of the period of the nature and character of the French bourgeoisie or workers, or of the distinctive behavior of humans of special genetic and biological traits, or human reactions under specific social conditions (126–27). Only those works that are conceived and developed strictly as literary works will last, believes Benet; the others will perish with the outdating of their information or *asunto*. Style and information are not equivalents of form and content. Benet distinguishes all these concepts from each other. Information, unlike content, is a more limited and more specific concept. One cannot class as information everything the writer says but only that which is said with a certain purpose of *docencia, docencia* meaning pedagogical or didactic intent, and showing something the author assumes the reader does not know (132). Form is far more limited than style, having to do with the structure of the sentence, selection of words, and modulation of meaning. Style covers much more, as indicated before. Under its control are not only all the forms of diction but also the detemporalization of information, that is, the transformation of particular information into an ever-lasting source of interest and enjoyment. The author's effort, Benet insists, should be geared to overcome with his style the extrinsic, accidental, temporal value of information; it should be calculated to extract from information that which is accidental and thus elaborate a different reality that will be permanent and always fascinating (140).

  Ambiguity and Certainty.   Throughout his essays Benet insists on the enigmatic nature of art and the logical clarity of science. In chapter two of *In Blossom*, "Incertidumbre, Memoria, Fatalidad y Temor" [Uncertainty, Memory, Fatality and Fear], Benet clearly outlines the nature of both the writer's and scientist's activities, their means of expression and the outcomes of their undertakings. The artist's or writer's function is to create literature with ambiguities as opposed to the scientist who seeks to develop a body of thought with categoric certainties (*In Blossom,* 44–45). Ambiguity in the literary work should be omnipresent, felt in the word, in the sentence, in the syntax, and in the general discourse. All of this should make it difficult to detect the main doctrine of the work, if it has any, and undermine its validity altogether. It is interesting to see how Benet admires Alonso de Ercillas's *La Araucana* precisely because of its ambivalence or ambiguity. Here he detects ambivalence in feelings and in structure, a structure that is epic and lyric, that follows the tenets of the epic poem but also deviates from it (*Door of Dust,* 18). In the same poetic discourse of the *Araucana* one finds concomitantly horror of war and admiration of courage, pride in conquest and scorn for domination, respect for the native and condemnation of idolatry and barbarism (*Door of Dust,* 18).

For the artist the world, nature, society, and man will always be enigmas and hence his art needs not to find solutions (*Door of Dust,* 45–48), a modesty that a man of science must repudiate because, unlike the former, the latter's mission is to work with reason, logic, and a systematic formula of expression in order to articulate clearly his discoveries. Contradiction, doubt, and ambivalence are the points of departure of the literary discourse as they are also the points where scientific discourse ends. The artist, according to Benet, moves toward the invention of mystery, mystery that will always remain beyond reason's reach. The scientist, on the other hand, seeks the revelation of mystery through a logical process of inquiry totally immune to the vagaries of chance, fatality, and fear, all of which stimulate the artist's lonely, creative activity.

In chapter six of *Inspiration and Style,* Benet devotes special attention to the mystery novel and the novel of the sea of the nineteenth century. He sees both as key deviations from the social novels of the period wherein imagination did not count and ambiguity was for all practical purposes nonexistent. Explaining the novel of the sea, Benet clearly indicates his admiration for the way the narrator of this type of novel builds mystery, for the way he makes mystery an end in itself, leaving the reader in confusion, with no keys to unlock that mystery. Interestingly enough, Benet, following this example, wrote his own novel of the sea, *Sub Rosa,* where the motives behind Basterra's crime are never known either by the narrator or by the surviving characters.

Metaphor-Hyperbole: Epic, Lyric Poetry, and the Chronicle. These five elements of rhetoric are dealt with in chapter one of *Door of Dust,* "Epica, Noética, Poética." The first distinction established by Benet in his discussion is between the epic poet and the chronicler. Both aim to tell or relate something, but in two different ways: the former follows the free impulse of his imagination and the latter the strict veracity of the story or the events. Being so, the epic poem entails a correct mode of writing and the chronicle, an exact way of telling. Correctness is necessary in order to translate the incredible and fabulous inventions of the epic imagination; exactness is needed in order accurately to follow the line of veracity required in the events recorded by the chronicler. The epic poet, limited only by his free imagination, is bound to relate unsuspected events that go beyond the ordinary and have a basic point of reference: man, his anger, his weakness, his ambitions, all seen through a magnifying and magnified perspective (*Door of Dust*, 20). Facts and events, this way, appear to be human even though they are superhuman. The epic poet feels the need to provide the reader with a scale of references between what he describes and what the reader knows from ordinary experience. That scale of reference marks the proportion between the epic, superhuman events and the reader's ordinary, human experience, to which he is accustomed (*Door of Dust*, 23). Hence the origin of metaphor. The epic poet must use a formula of speech whereby he can explain the superhuman reality through the ordinary world or experience of the reader, which is the purpose of metaphor. In a metaphor, the *tenor* is grasped by the reader through the intelligibility of the *vehicle* (Benet uses precisely I. A. Richards's famous terminology for exploring the metaphoric phenomenon). As the epic poet transforms the extraordinary into the ordinary, the lyric poet transforms the ordinary into the extraordinary. And in order to do it, the former resorts to metaphor, the latter to hyperbole (*Door of Dust*, 43). Both metaphor and hyperbole entail an analogy between two elements, the "comparable" and the "compared." In a regular metaphor the "comparable" element is an object of the imagination and the "compared" an object of reality (tenor-imagination-vehicle-reality). When this analogy is inverted, that is, when the poet uses an object of reality as the "comparable" element and an object of the imagination as the "compared" element of the analogy, then we have the case of hyperbole normally employed, says Benet, by the lyric poet.

This process of "hyperbolization" can become so intense that what seems to be an identifiable reality (used as part of the analogy) is an already transformed entity that few will understand since the point of departure or the original base upon which the metaphoric layering is built (vehicle) is already a metaphor. This is the case of Góngora's famous "metaphoric metaphorization" prevalent in seventeenth-century Spain as well as among some poets of the brilliant group of 1927. Obviously, what he has to say on these topics is not original but does reveal a clear understanding of the writer's many rhetorical devices and of the intricacies encountered in the creative process.

Poetry and History. Benet uses this Aristotelean distinction in order to arrive at his own conclusion concerning the function of the poet and that of the historian. He explains why one is more "serious," "sublime," and "truthful" than the other. Both inform the reader about something, but while the historian is left with the veracity and interest of the events he narrates, the poet goes beyond, in search of a new reality not only unknown to him but also a "reality" which may not even exist (*Inspiration,* 166). As he searches for the unknown the poet must work with uncertainties, vagueness, mere suggestions and even contradictions, a situation avoided by the historian. One may say—adds Benet—that while the poet invents a reality, the historian re-creates that which already exists (*Inspiration,* 168).

The Literary Work and the Critic. Benet conceives a true work of art as an independent object, an original and solid individuality defined exclusively by style. It is not *another* social or cultural product but an individual product of an individual style. And the critic, avers Benet, must delve into that individual work, try to explain its mystery and nothing else. He rejects the critic who, by conceiving the work of art as another cultural or social product, wastes his time looking for influences, origins of styles, and the like. This "anthropologic" critic is destined to remain outside the work, never to taste and enjoy its inner mystery (*In Blossom,* 85–90).

Theory of Language

The Angel of the Lord Abandons Tobit is a collection of seven essays dealing primarily with linguistics and, to a lesser degree, with literary and visual expressions, as well as grammatical, religious, philosophical, and sociopolitical ideas insofar as they are related to the realm of language. For his long, intricate, and at times tedious discussions, Benet uses as concrete evidence to back up his ideas two fundamental works: the biblical story of Tobit and those works of Rembrandt based on and inspired by Tobit's story, seven oil

paintings and a total of twelve drawings and engravings, all produced between 1626 and 1660. The biblical story serves Benet for
his linguistic analysis, with Rembrandt's works as visual aids accompanying the discussions. Of special importance in the book is
the artist's famous oil *The Angel of the Lord Abandons Tobit,* used in
the first essay to illustrate the distinction and difference between
the synchronic expression of visual objects and the diachronic itin-
erary of the sentence or text, along with their respective intellection
or perception (28–29).

Benet's first major contention is that the *signified* of a *signifier* is
not a concept, a thought, or an idea, as Saussure maintained, but
the signifier itself, which is to say, the word itself. This means that
the use of any sign refers to the word, and the word remits to itself
(42). If this is the case, then the word becomes the final destiny of
thought, not vice versa. Words do conceptualize, but at the same
time—adds Benet—concepts do not speak in general. By speaking
he means not the formal expression of a given sign, known in
advance, but rather the combination of several of them (signs), joined
together to complete or consolidate a *new* formula. The intrinsic
value and independence of the word or sign runs parallel to the
concept's paralyzing function. This linguistic conception is aptly
put to work in *In the State,* where the word (or the sign) is the means
and the end in itself, where content or concept totally recedes in
order for the word to take command.

Inspired by the spirit of linguistic freedom and the preeminence
of the word, Benet does not hesitate to show and ridicule the futility
he finds in some "guardians" of language whose disciplines strive
to limit its growth and the freedom of those who use it. He aims
his darts especially at linguists and grammarians. About the linguist's scientific investigation Benet says that "the more it discovers,
the more it [the investigation] removes them [the linguists] from
the possibility of reaching the ultimate foundation of science" (67).
Since subject matter or the body of investigation of linguistics is
modifiable and everchanging, it is only logical that it will never be
subjected to an inflexible normative control. Linguistics—continues
Benet—"like Geomorphology, will be as appealing as it is ineffec-
tive, as subjective as it is inoperative, as revealing of details as it
is incapable of formulating one single law of general validity" (67).
The same can be said of grammarians, as they are in charge of the
"correct" usage of language despite the crucial fact that many aspects

of it will never be reduced to their laws. Time, for example, says Benet, will always be a mystery to grammar; and verbs as a consequence will never be totally subject to grammatical rules. Distinctions between absolute and relative tenses or perfect and imperfect are only arbitrary. It is not a matter of distinguishing absolute or relative terms but of establishing the degree of precision or imprecision inherent in a particular verb form (152–53). Unlike the linguist or the grammarian, the poet, the writer, or the literary creator has a mysterious instrument, his style, his work, with which to delve into all the categories of absolute time in an effort to rationalize its mystery, the mystery of "absolute time, that is and is not, that is everything and is going to be nothing or something, that was everything and hardly is anything; that which is left from it already was, is not what it was . . . it is only a part of what it is, so that a part of what it is, is part of what it was, and that which will be, etc." (146). It is through this linguistic maze that the writer captures time's enigma. Language is the poet's vast dominion, his realm for self-realization. No one can strip the writer of his privilege to use language as he wishes, ignoring the regulations issued by its "guardians" (130). And just for pure pleasure, he allows those whom he disdains to nurture themselves with his precious food (language):

> Out idle words, servants to shallow fools,
> Unprofitable sounds, weak arbitrators
> Busy yourselves in skill-contending schools,
> Debate where leisure serves with dull debaters;
> To trembling clients be you mediators:
> For me, I force not argument a straw,
> Since that my case is past the help of law. (130)

Like the lonely linguist searching for the ultimate scientific foundation for his discipline, the philosopher also searches for "the truth" without realizing that truth is not a rule, a category of judgment, or a principle of science but a lonely surprise or an unsuspected reality. A truth—not *the* truth—as a surprise implies that to find it is a fortuitous act, an accident, never a calculated, regulated achievement. The philosopher is always eager to find the very mine or source of truth and formulate the way to find it (121). Obviously, this is an arrogant hope which drastically contrasts with that of the writer, who finds partial truth but never formulates how (121). His search is never planned. A truth is more likely to be found through a broken, chaotic discourse than through a systematic, logical formula of expression. The writer finds truth—affirms Benet—at the end of a senseless prolongation of language led by a frenetic "horse of words" that seems to be heading toward error but suddenly hits a star, unveiling a "luminous corner" of unsuspected truth (121). Truth is mysterious and so is the writer's means of approaching it and, hopefully, finding it. Once it is found, he cannot formulate how he did it or ultimately define what truth really is. His response to life, language, mystery, or truth is impulsive, instinctive, and irrational—never calculated (97–99).

Again, the importance of the book stems not from the novelty, variety, or profundity of the ideas or even the way the discussions are presented, but from the extrinsic fact that it does help further to understand Benet's literary creation, especially since the book is a theoretical anticipation of his latest novelistic experiment *In The State,* where language ceases to be a means and becomes an end in itself, where the sign, the word, does not refer to a concept, but reverts to itself.

More on Culture, Science, and Art

Benet's latest essay of significance for the understanding of his literary production has been included in his book *Of the Well and of Numa,* which is divided into two parts, the essay itself and the legend wherein the main character is El Numa, the same destructive and mythical force appearing in most of Benet's fiction set in Región. Benet divides this essay into three connected discussions dealing with (1) culture, science, and art; (2) Thomas Mann and his main works; and (3) Thomas Mann's tetralogy, *Joseph and His Brothers,* in relation to its biblical counterpart.

Benet contends that "Culture has not always run parallel with society. Today, yes; today culture does nothing else but to accompany the evolution of society, subject to a science that, at the most, forestalls the tools that will satisfy, for a short period of time, the needs of that evolution" (13). Cultural evolution is no longer a spiritual evolution. Its steps are utterly controlled by a scientific mind which must respond to the material needs of an ever-growing society, alien and at times hostile to any spiritual mystery. Since it is the scientist who rules and determines the evolutionary process of society, it is inevitable that the role of the poet, the visionary, will become more and more underrated. The poet's concern is not sociological but eschatological. He seeks the mysterious, not the concrete, creating a world in which nothing is certain but all is questionable and enigmatic, like man's own destiny (17). Since the poet does not believe in any truth, he cannot prove anything and, since he cannot prove anything, he cannot produce categorical formulae. This being so, he will never enjoy the approving consensus of society and will never strive for it either, since he knows that any effort in that direction is futile (18). His situation is both that of an orphan and of a hero, since his mission is alien to the rest of society, i.e., to that informed mass who live under the rules of social and religious conformity and have "renounced forever the adventure of the spirit into the unknown and into that which is vigorously mysterious" (14). These ideas of course are not original, yet they are useful, helping to understand Benet's personality and also his novelistic world which is built precisely on enigma and paradox, never conforming to any novelistic rule or formula. His is a world where nothing is certain, where everything is an approximation leading nowhere.

This preliminary discussion affords Benet the opportunity to study Thomas Mann's personality and works, and specifically the famed tetralogy, *Joseph and His Brothers*. Benet finds in Mann's novel a systematic, semiscientific, and mathematical expansion of the thirty-page biblical source. Fifty pages of Mann—says Benet—correspond to one of the thirty from the biblical story, a total then of 1,500 pages. Mann worked within a plan already preestablished by the original story, which he carefully expanded with a detailed psychological analysis of each character. This made the work a psychological treatise lacking the ambiguity and other characteristics of an authentic product of poetic invention (75). Benet's argumentation to condemn the novelistic shallowness and weakness of Mann's works fails to be convincing for many reasons: (1) Most of his discussions of the novel and the biblical story are vague generalizations of linguistic and stylistic virtuosity but of very little analytical substance. Indeed the linguistic pattern of his essay resembles very much the capriciously long, ambiguous sentences of his Numa legend, and of his other books of fiction. (2) One has to question the validity of Benet's method, that of relating Mann's novel to the biblical story. Why not approach Mann's *Joseph and His Brothers* exclusively through *Joseph and His Brothers?* Benet fails to see Mann's novel as an independent, self-sufficient, and autonomous work of art that, in order to weigh its literary value, one should analyze by itself. It seems that Benet here is acting precisely as the "anthropologic" critic he condemned in his earlier essays. (3) To try to see the work as a bourgeois product, tuned to the general status quo, simply because the author was bourgeois, is certainly an oversimplification. And Benet does this by using his preliminary discussions on culture, science, and art as an ideological background against which he places critically Mann's personality and work.

Chapter Four

The Theater:
The Uncertain Stage

Benet's collected literary output in the realm of the theater consists of three interesting plays published in 1971 in a book titled *Teatro*. [1] They are *Anastas o el Origen de la Constitución* [Anastas or The Origin of the Constitution], *Agonía Confutans,* and *Un caso de conciencia* [A Case of Consciousness]. They were written in 1958, 1966, and 1967, respectively. As a whole, *Teatro* already exhibits the use of some of Benet's major stylistic and technical devices, later implemented with greater emphasis and skill in the major works of fiction. Among those devices, the following stand out: (1) the subtle juxtaposition of reality and fantasy as a means to create an intricate world of ambiguity and uncertainty *(A Case of Consciousness);* (2) the use of long, exhausting, and uninhibited sentences to bring out the characters' tormented inner selves; (3) the frequent use of dialogues (indeed, more than dialogues, they are long and lonely monologues) filled with numerous digressions and contradictions that destroy quite abruptly the normal flow and continuity of the main line of thought *(Agonía Confutans);* (4) the special manipulation of characters who, more than individuals of flesh and bone, are mere voices, or *sombras,* spectral creatures bottled in their own futility and nothingness; and (5) the recurrence of the typical Benet tendency to sabotage the genre to which the respective work belongs; some of his dramas are stripped of the traditional dramatic components. For instance, some have no stage directions or stage at all *(Agonía Confutans),* making the staging impossible, or at least very difficult. According to Benet, only his more traditional play *Anastas or The Origin of the Constitution* has been staged twice, once in Madrid and another time in Murcia. [2] It must be noted that important themes reappearing in his latter works are also found in these plays. They include the antithetical conflict between instinct (passion) and reason; the conception of mystery as an essential component of literary reality; the futility of man's attempt to explain his existence and his ontological loneliness; and the conception of time as a mere repetition of misfortunes. Man is viewed here basically as a suffering creature with no hope of overcoming that state of being.

Anastas o el origen de la Constitución [Anastas or The Origin of the Constitution]

Anastas or The Origin of the Constitution is a political farce of deception, terror, and death. Sometime in the *época actual* ("present time") a ridiculous and caricaturesque king named Anastas (a syllabic inversion of the word Satanás) utterly bored and never sure of himself or of his ability to rule his kingdom—most likely Spain—decides to draw up a constitution that would protect him and his throne against the ambitions of his associates and the imminent rebellion of his people. Five of his most trusted ministers, Ruytelán, Tioda, Micaure, Caucas, and Stratos, are assigned to this legislative task, which is absurdly carried out in the midst of rivalries, jealousies, and death. Four ministers are eliminated by the king under the opportune advice of his right-hand man, Stratos, the evil mastermind who eventually stabs the king to usurp the throne and make use of the new constitution for his own benefit. The structural symmetry of the play is activated by a periodic succession of crimes and by the recurrence of key images that endow the work with unity through multiple levels of reality.

To suggest both the cyclical inevitability of political chaos and the futility of power, the play opens and closes with similar dramatic situations where an incapable ruler is preparing to rule; at the beginning, that ruler is Anastas and at the end, Stratos. The sole witness of the two is Gaspar, the indifferent servant who secretly knows the gloomy destiny of his masters (death) and of his nation (chaos). In addition to Gaspar, each ruler is reminded of his precarious power, criminal mistakes, and the consequences by the shadows of their predecessors, Anastas by the shadow of Phocas and Stratos by the shadow of Anastas, a key dramatic device endowing the play and the rulers with two levels of reality: the conscious reality of their actual political power and the subconscious guilt surrounding its origin. The nagging, recurrent presence of the shadows undermines the peace of mind and tranquility of each ruler to the extent that their power more than a source of personal happiness becomes a permanent hell in which each one is doomed to live (21, 26, 51, 60). Phocas's shadow says to Anastas: "the tradition of political crime continues; power rests only in you. And it can only be exhibited by he who with his own hands does away with your existence. Good-bye, Anastas. The days left for you are numbered. Your death is being prepared with utmost caution" (37). Similar words are uttered by Anastas's shadow to Stratos: ". . . the tradition of political crime continues, only through crime is the crown won. You already know what is waiting for you, assassin" (77). The rulers do not mold history for they are only the passive agents and continuers of a tradition marked by political crime and deception, appearing in the play and in life as mere puppets with no freedom or personal honor. They are victims of tradition and of their own ambition and blindness. Even the violent and bloody way they kill each other is already molded and patterned by tradition (38, 39, 76, 77); they neither can nor want to deviate from it. The audience sees both how Phocas's blood becomes Anastas's, which eventually will become Stratos's, and how the same sword is used by each, followed by the water of innocence drawn from the faucet to wash their bloodstained hands.

Since force is the means to achieve power, law and order do not count. And any attempt to obey is simply a false pretense employed by the ruler both to minimize rebellion and popular discontent and to make his personal ambition appear a disinterested and democratic endeavor (40). Compatible with this mockery of law is the drawing of the constitution itself, whose only article is geared to save the king, disregarding totally the interests and well-being of his people (70–71). Since force is the origin of the king's power, it is logical that the constitution should seek his protection and the elimination of force, a goal that is not reached, for the king is at the end the victim precisely of his own "legal" precautions.

Stylistically, the play moves in two different yet complementary directions: on the one hand, toward a direct, visible, more real perspective and, on the other, toward a more subconscious, absurd, distorting vision of the world of politics, which obviously enhances the overall effect of the play and definitely redeems it from being another of those amateur political dramatic pamphlets so common in the new Spanish theater. This does not mean, however, that this piece is as rich and innovative as are most of Benet's works of prose fiction. Far from it; it lacks subtlety, ambiguity, and dramatic effectiveness.

As noted, the play is a farce wherein the characters, rather than real human beings acting with freedom, are distorted puppets, over-whelmed by the predicaments of tradition, passion, and *sinrazón* ("unreason"). Since reason is absent in the life of these people, what they say and do is a nonsensical proposition, part of their nonsensical behavior. For the well-being of his kingdom, Anastas proposes the elimination of agriculture, commerce, and industry while encouraging a policy of isolation with the "consequent" need to rebuild the armed forces (58). The great politician's secret of success rests, says Anastas to his servant Gaspar, "on making people believe that one is deceiving them so that the people in turn may do that which they think they should not do, trying thus to deceive me and not doing what I precisely do not want them to do" (18–19). Before letting his ministers into the meeting room Anastas instructs Gaspar:

Take Tioda aside and tell him to wait until everyone else has left. On the stairs tell Ruytelán that upon reaching the front door he should turn around and come upstairs making sure that no one sees him. Tell Caucas to move away from Ruytelán for awhile and to tell Stratos to watch over Tioda. Tell Stratos for me not to pay attention to Caucas and to come with Micaure to me immediately. And tell Micaure to escape from both Stratos and Tioda and to put himself in contact with Ruytelán. Have you understood, Gaspar? (20)

This nonsensical labyrinth of orders generates an oneiric atmosphere of confusion, insecurity, and chaos in the characters' actions and in the drama itself. Laughter is the reader's or audience's main reaction. Quite appropriate is the way the characters appear on stage. The king, dragging his feet and carrying on his head a large "gross" crown made of *latón* ("brass"), grabs a mosquito off his face and brings it to his mouth. Grotesquely, his ministers rush to his room, tripping on each other like a troupe of clowns in a circus, the worn-out rags they wear matching the distorted configuration of their faces and personalities. The synchronic and mechanical elimination of the characters through error and gross injustice adequately fits their puppetlike, mechanic condition and absurdist vision of power and existence.

Agonía Confutans

Agonía Confutans is a "dramatic" piece divided into two acts and a Prologue. The Prologue is presented by a character known as *El Censor* ("The Censor"), who reappears in Act I but later disappears in Act II. In the Prologue, *El Censor,* adopting an authorial posture of ironic undertones and cognizant of the nature and spirit of the work of which he is part, proclaims: "In view of the growing difficulties offered by the business of the theater, we have decided to simplify many things. Thus, for greater clarity and better comprehension of the representation, the continuity of the scenes has been eliminated. Therefore, these scenes are developed according to an order, even though this is an arbitrary one" (81). He explains that the work's nature is inconsequential, as is the order in which the acts are arranged. The reader therefore may choose to read first Act I or Act II. He indicates that for this dialogue's success, the presence or absence of the audience makes no difference, and concludes his Prologue by warning the reader or audience of the many contradictions, confusions, and difficulties inherent in the subject and nature of the characters' discussion. This seemingly unimportant introduction generates a variety of artistic and formal effects: (1) *El Censor,* although a character, adopts the position of the author when he explains the full "nature of the work" and the reason for its particular present form. Furthermore, he knows in advance that the *work will* be developed according to an arbitrary order. (2) When he says: "we have decided to simplify many things," it seems that he and the other two characters, not the author, are solely responsible for the actual creation of the work, that is, for its specific content and its unique delivery and structure. For all practical purposes the author, Benet, has nothing to do with the play and his participation is "eliminated" from the creative process. (3) From what *El Censor* says in the Prologue and does in Act I, it is safe to suggest that his only role in the dialogue is that of a simple moderator, a witness to the other two characters' long, tedious debate, a point leading us to conclude that only Corpus and Pertes should be accountable for what they say and how they arrange their ideas. And consequently, neither Benet nor *El Censor* has anything to do with it— a magnificent, double detachment that sets up from the beginning the ironic tone prevalent throughout the work.

Agonía Confutans is a long, tedious dialogue wherein two entities, Corpus and Pertes (perhaps representing the Body and the Spirit), engage in a calculated discussion of a variety of topics such as freedom, love, happiness, the relationship between man and the cosmos and between man and his fellow men, etc. As one must expect, the conclusion is that all of man's enigmas have no solution and that his perpetual solitude is a hell from which he cannot escape (144–46). And that hell is also for the two of them, for Pertes and for Corpus. The former says, toward the end of the futile dialogue: "Let us not deceive ourselves, it is useless to deceive. The solitude in which I live is a hell." And the latter adds: "It is also for me. But your company is also a hell." Pertes replies: "It is also for me. And knowing how mine is for you, I chose solitude to avoid greater unhappiness [*sinsabores*]" (144). The result is the same for Corpus's bitter existence or for Pertes's happiness since the former feels and later fully acknowledges that his unhappiness every day is bound never to cease and never to reach an end; and the latter feels and also acknowledges that his happiness is only a small part of a total happiness he will never be able to obtain (119). The torment they experience stems from their personal, inherent incapability to conquer the complete and total state of unhappiness or happiness respectively (120). The dialogue is only a means to kill time and, as such, a mere acting to cover their existential, never-ending agony and solitude (97).

The dialogue here is stripped of all the conventional mechanics normally associated with the drama. There are references neither to time nor space. There are no stage directions or, for that matter, any stage at all. The characters are only somber voices with no apparent sign of visual presence. And the dramatic action is substituted by the tension stemming from the subtle exchange of ideas, from their development and from the persuasiveness of the argumentation conducted by the characters, leading them to the question of who needs whom: does Corpus need Pertes or vice versa? Later they delve into other enigmas with no solution. From the form and content of the dialogue, the play resembles Benet's future fictional writings, especially the section of *You Will Return to Región* where Dr. Sebastián sustains a lengthy and futile dialogue with Gamallo's daughter, thus evincing the uninterrupted evolution of Benet's stylistic method.

Un caso de conciencia [A Case of Consciousness]

If one were to classify this work, one would say that it is a psychological play: man's consciousness is the main area of exploration, as the title clearly reveals. To explore it, Benet uses two conflicting characters, Mr. Arnau, a wealthy widower from a southern Spanish province, and his daughter, Carmen, a sexually frustrated woman who, married to Julián, prefers adultery for two reasons: (1) to convince herself of her freedom and (2) to test her individual strength and ability to cope with some of her adultery's consequences, which are the loneliness wherein she is found when Julián leaves her, the subsequent illusion of his return, and the strange feeling she experiences at home, alone, with her father, who sees in her some kind of tacit substitute for his wife. Other characters included in the list of *Personae* are Adela, the maid, and the *Guarda*'s Shadow. Other characters not included in the list but often mentioned throughout are the man in the country eating figs, the *cónsul*, De Bastos, who seems to be Carmen's lover, and Elena, her sister. In view of the complex maze of existing feelings in the father and his daughter, the preceding interpretation is only an approximation. Indeed, the reader may be able to formulate many other interpretations, as is the case in Benet's more mature works of fiction (this play was written the same year in which *You Will Return to Región* was published). By his skillfully juxtaposing reality with fiction and by eliminating all barriers between them, the reader (or audience) is forced to remain in a permanent state of uncertainty concerning what is happening on the stage and in the heart and consciousness of the father and his daughter. The same uncertainty is detected in the characters' relationship with each other, since what they say often contradicts what they think. The contradiction is revealed to the audience through the dramatic device of the *aparte* ("aside").

The first major problem encountered is whether or not Julián actually returns or is simply another *Sombra,* like the *Guarda*'s, included in the list of characters. Is Julián dead? If so, who killed him: perhaps Mr. Arnau, or even his daughter? Is the man eating figs the *cónsul,* De Bastos, or Julián himself? Does Elena, who is not included among the *Personae* of the play, really exist or is she only a projection of Carmen's sexual desire to have Julián as she had him when he was only her fiancé? Is the *Guarda* the person for whom she deceived her husband and for that reason the latter (Ju-

lián) presumably killed the former (the *Guarda*)? This host of ambiguities, more than enhancing the play as a spectacle, undermines
its dramatic effectiveness, leaving the work as a good exploration
of the inner conflicts of the self, but nothing more. And the same
can be said of the other plays, especially of *Agonía Confutans,* whose
dialogue is devoid of all dramatic illusion.[3]

One cannot fail, however, to see in the last play a sharp criticism
of the Spanish concept of sex, wherein reason overwhelms the senses.
That is, sex as a function is subject to an inflexible reason that
resorts to marriage to allow satisfaction. Its parody is obvious here
when one realizes that marriage leads Carmen into unhappiness.
And in order to overcome it she chooses to be unfaithful. By being
unfaithful, however, she creates problems for her inner, psychological self. Again, this is another of Benet's labyrinths: Carmen enters
without realizing that there is no exit.

Chapter Five
The Novelette:
Entering the Labyrinth

Benet's six novelettes are chronologically scattered throughout his entire career: from his first and seminal four-work collection, *Nunca llegarás a nada* [You Will Never Get Anywhere], dating back to the 1950s, up to his latest legend, "Numa," published in 1978 as part of *Del pozo y del Numa (un ensayo y una leyenda)* [Of the Well and Numa (an essay and a legend)]. In between, two important pieces were published: *Una tumba* [A Tomb] in 1971 and "Sub Rosa" in 1973, the latter being included in a book of short stories bearing the same title. The novelettes as a whole clearly reveal Benet's poetic imagination and narrative versatility.

You Will Never Get Anywhere is Benet's first formal step into literary creation, a collection of four novelettes written between 1958 and 1961, when the group was published. A second edition of the collection appeared in 1969, the same year Benet was awarded the *Biblioteca Breve* Literary Prize for his second novel, *A Meditation*. The second edition of *You Will Never Get Anywhere* differs slightly from the first, which the author later termed a "superficial and dully written" work,[1] a statement not to be taken seriously, for the stories are quite the opposite. They are well-built, well-written pieces that, had Benet not written anything else, by themselves would have placed him among the most original narrators in Spanish Literature.[2] But most important, *You Will Never Get Anywhere* is in many respects Benet's seminal work. Many stylistic and thematic characteristics prevalent in his later works are visible in these early novelettes. Of special importance are his typical long, exhausting sentences, the enigmatic nature of characters, the consistent minimization of plot, the emergence of his mythical Región along with its ruins and overwhelming solitude, and man's inevitable failure embodied in one of Benet's most important images, that of the journey, which

man must begin, even if he knows it will lead nowhere. The novelettes of *You Will Never Get Anywhere* are "Nunca llegarás a nada"
[You Will Never Get Anywhere], "Baalbec, una mancha" [Baalbec,
a Stain], "Duelo" [Mourning], and "Después" [Afterwards].

The Title Tale: "You Will Never Get Anywhere"

Juan, the protagonist, recounts a trip taken in the past with
Vicente, his wealthy friend, through northern Europe: France, Ger-
many, Denmark, and other unspecified countries. His recollection
covers the period of preparation and the trip itself. The mystery
which clouds the story is progressively intensified with the detailed
and introspective description of events. This description, however,
is carried out not because of the events as such, but rather because
of their metaphysical implications which enable Juan to evolve and
elucidate his own conception of life and his vision of the world.
The plot of the work, therefore, does not rest on the dynamic
sequence of those events in time, but instead on their inner human
value that motivates the character's search for himself and for his
place in the world. Thus, the trip to northern Europe is a symbol
of man's odyssey into himself. The more detailed it is, the more
complete his concept of life becomes. Taking into account the development of the plot, this short story is a novelette that opens with
what structurally constitutes its conclusion: the sketch of a drunken
Englishman and what he says about the two traveling friends. After
asking them why they force themselves to continue traveling aim-
lessly, he says that they are poor humans trying in vain to survive,
"trying to rise again" (9–10). Acknowledging the truth of these
statements (after the journey, but at the beginning of the narrative),
remarks which when they were made had no meaning to either of
them, Juan says somewhat regretfully that "we ignored him" (9).
In the closing pages, the reader learns that the Englishman also said
(consistent with what he has already stated about man) that "this
common body, like to a vagabond flag upon the stream, goes to
and back, lackeying the varying tide, to rot itself with motion"
(63). The part of the English sentence which imporessed Juan the
most was "to rot itself with motion." He is not sure about the
construction of the enigmatic language in which, he felt later, the
truth was hidden. So in order to reveal it, measure its scope, as if
impelled by the inner desire for self-definition, he must start the

recollection of his symbolic journey. It should be realized that what his anonymous friend had to say is reproduced defectively, thus emphasizing the fallibility and the efforts to grasp the truth embodied in the English statement.

The artistic complexity derived from the Englishman's statements is unique and important to the total structure of the work, for the following reasons. (1) From a novelistic point of view, Juan recalls his journey and thus this novelette is created. He knows where and when it started and ended. From a metaphysical point of view, he is in the same situation as the reader; he is about to embark and does not know his destination. It is the tension between these two realities that enhances the artistic beauty of the work. Such a tension originates from the uncertainty of the character about the where and the when of the events. There is a "fluid time," says Juan, that links and separates all events in our life. No one knows what occurs in that time; no one is able to remember the past or foresee the future (24–25). Juan does not remember when and from where he went to Paris (24). The reader knows from the Englishman that man's voyage in life will lead nowhere, yet he insists on reading the work, that is, binding himself to continue with Juan's self-discovery, which is also his own. (2) Thus, the reader and the protagonist, who shows him the way to nothingness, at the end become the drunken Englishman, both able to reach the same conclusion about themselves. (3) Juan and the reader follow in the footsteps of the Englishman, whom they unfortunately ignored and whose words—"you will never get anywhere"—they did not heed. (4) Ironically, the truth given at the beginning is the truth found and experienced at the end. In addition, that same loose truth of the beginning becomes at the end the unifying element which circularly structures the work, which is seemingly formless. This circular structure is aesthetically satisfying since the idea of an odyssey is developed. The actual destination of both the character and the reader becomes their point of departure: nothingness. One may say that if they reached nothingness, philosophically, they got somewhere. But that somewhere, in the poetic context of the work, means nothingness, which in the final analysis is nowhere, and hence the title of the work. This thematic and artistic vicious circle is another aspect that makes Benet's literature an essentially enigmatic experience. It is worth noting here that this title is poetically significant to the spirit and artistic expression of the content it embodies. The double negative in the Spanish (*nunca llegarás a nada*) alludes to the ubiquity of man's nothingness in time and space as seen through the protagonist.

Benet's preoccupation with the traditional concepts of time and character in "You Will Never Get Anywhere" is minimal. These two technical elements are subject to the total vision of the work revealed through the inner reality of Juan. Character and time, rather than ends in themselves, are only means to the end of novelistic architecture. The flow of Juan's recollection of events emanates from his obsession with the search for himself and not from the chronological sequence of their actual occurrence in the past. This is one of the reasons why the reader may experience difficulty in following the trend of thought and reflection wrought by the dense narration of the story.

"Baalbec, a Stain"

Again a central character relates a trip, this one a return to his hometown, Región, the mythical place Benet will continue to use as a setting for his main novels. The protagonist's longings to visit the land of his childhood, and particularly his mother's tomb, become a moral necessity when he receives a letter from Ramón Fernández Huesca urging him to come to help in settling a dispute over the property lines of his terrain, Burrero. That dispute has been raised by the mysterious character Miss Cordón, who claims to have inherited the land from her mother. Huesca believes Burrero was originally purchased from the protagonist's grandmother by a Mr. Faber, and from him by Huesca. According to Miss Cordón's papers, her mother, Eulalia Cordón, had the legal right to the same lot since Blanca Servén de Benzal, the protagonist's grandmother, upon borrowing twelve thousand pesetas from Miss Cordón's mother, committed herself to transfer Burrero to the lender (85). These are the external and clearly developed elements of the story's plot.

There are, however, other hidden pieces, revealed by suggestion, that complete this literary mosaic. Part of the artistic success of the novella rests on the pieces themselves as well as on the skillful way they are scattered and organized. The two seemingly unimportant references which unlock the enigma of "Baalbec, a Stain" are the flowers given by the protagonist to Miss Cordón for her parents' tomb and the initial "E" on the Indian-made clay pot found in her room. The flowers were given to Miss Cordón upon his arrival in Región; to his surprise he found them later on the tomb of his own family when he decided to honor their memory by leaving flowers there also. The initial engraved on the Indian pot stands for Enrique Benzal. Miss Cordón, therefore, is Enrique's daughter. The last paragraph states that the twelve thousand pesetas became the price Blanca Servén de Benzal received for her sick son (Enrique Benzal) from his demented mistress (Eulalia Cordón) (116).

The consequences of this plot development are numerous and morally significant. Not only did Blanca Servén de Benzal cheat Eulalia Cordón and Mr. Faber by selling the same property twice, but she also deceived her own granddaughter (Miss Cordón). The moral consequences of her actions perhaps did not constitute the author's primary concern, but they are essential to the concepts of destruction and ruin, the major theme not only of this story but of much of Benet's other fiction as well. The downfall of the protagonist's town and family is the symbol of modern society's physical and moral destruction, and hence the title: "Baalbec, a Stain." Baalbec is the site of ruins of ancient Heliopolis and the "stain" is the moral decadence that is part of the ruins. Throughout the story a succession of ruins, reminiscent of man's life, is suggested. The family's main house was built on the debris of another one, just as Huesca's future is to be founded on the Benzals' ruins. In the solidity and strength of the walls, one is to foresee the moisture of destruction and solitude (71–81). All of León Benzal Ordóñez's dreams and efforts (his name means lion) to build and leave a strong family for posterity were self-destructive, for nothingness was the sole permanent reality left at the end.

One of the key points in understanding and appreciating the aesthetic and moral scope of this work is found in the answer to this question: Why does the protagonist tell the facts, reactions, and experiences of his trip in such an ambiguous, enigmatic, and confusing way? To attempt to answer this, one must analyze and evaluate his role as narrator, sensitive to what he says and how he says it, and his present opinion of what he narrates; that is, the way he thinks and feels about the incidents now, after his trip. He is embarrassed about what his family has done to the helpless Eulalia Cordón and consequently to his cousin (Miss Cordón). His embarrassment forces him to relate to the reader its cause in a puzzlelike manner so that it would be as difficult to perceive as it was for him when he was in Región. The reader's experience in finding the truth in the work reflects the protagonist's experience in finding the truth in reality. Both had to put the pieces together in order to find sense in the nonsense of the events. There are three causes for his embarrassment: (1) he knows how his once morally rigid family was stained and the nature of that stain; (2) Huesca and Miss Cordón know about this stigma; and (3) they know he is aware of their knowledge of what has occurred in his family. The irony in all this is that his original nostalgic desire to go back to his family's past leads him to disappointment and further confirmation of the stupidity and nonsense of life. Second, instead of helping Huesca solve his problems with Miss Cordón, the protagonist complicates them even further.

As was said earlier, the reader's experience in finding the truth in the work constitutes a reflection of the protagonist's experience in finding the truth in reality (Región). To assess the consequences of this artistic parallel, it is necessary to determine why the central character—indeed the creator of himself—has to release all the information about his family problem. After explaining her legal rights to Burrero, Miss Cordón insinuatingly says to Huesca and the protagonist, "I just wanted you two to know all this" (87). For the protagonist, this statement becomes a painful reminder of the moral responsibility inherited from his family. He says, "I felt the weight of embarrassment to which Huesca was the witness" (87). But he cannot do anything about it. Henceforth, his peace of mind is undermined by this guilt feeling. To relieve himself of this tormenting responsibility, he is impelled to confess it to the reader, and he does so in exactly the same way he experienced the reality being confessed: in a puzzlelike manner. The exactness of his perception (Región) and expression (the book) of reality, the character's reality, to him is an honest way of presenting the truth, but to the reader it is a deceptive one. The impression left is that he tries to hide the truth under the paradoxical, confusing organization of events and their reasoning. The aesthetic value of this rests, however, on the confrontation between the protagonist and the reader and between the former's reality and the latter's fiction, the fiction he holds in his hands: "Baalbec, a Stain."

"Mourning"

In this work ruin or destruction is again Benet's thematic concern. The action takes place in Región, the gloomy town of death, deception, and oblivion with which Benet's readers are already familiar.

The four characters the author plays with to develop that theme are Lucas, his squirelike Blanco, Amelia, and Rosa. There may be indeed only two, for the lives of Lucas and Amelia seem to be enfolded in those of Blanco and Rosa, the male-female symbolic duality that strives for love but instead finds death. The ambiguity of plot construction, character development, and time structure is once again the essence of Benet's novelistic architecture. It is perhaps in this work, more than in any other of this collection, where Benet's efforts to achieve enigmatic literature reach the highest degree of intensity. What is left of conventional reality is symbolically no more than its vestiges on which a new poetic reality is built. Its effects can only be felt intuitively, rather than logically explained. Irony, Benet's central device to expose the tragic sense, or rather nonsense, of life, is, in "Mourning," integrated in the mainstream of the plot, in the subversive wielding of love, not as a means to life but to death and nothingness, the resulting reality for Rosa and for those who, after her death, were plunged into the eternal mourning suggested by the title. The enfolding of Lucas and Amelia in the lives of Blanco and Rosa enables Benet to create the cyclical pattern of destruction, since the secret relations of the younger couple are the projection of the Lucas-Amelia relationship which leads them nowhere.

"Afterwards"

"Afterwards," the last tale of the collection, commences, as do the others, with the description of the isolation and deterioration of the house and the lethargy and annihilation of the people who live in it. The house mentioned here is not where the father lived, but where his son is secluded. The frequent reminiscences of past grandeur of the family's hopes about the future serve to contrast, with severe irony, the hyperbolic nature of those dreams and the intensity of destruction inherent in the present reality (182). The three main characters, who, like shadows of themselves, float in this somber reality, are the father, the son, and the son's aged tutor. The plot is minimal: friends of the deceased father arrange and perform his burial, which the son at first refuses, but later is forced, to attend. They return to the father's house to work on the papers the dead man has left. The son is transferred to the other house where he was previously isolated by his father (for a supposed crime the father later learned never occurred) and where he will finally die. The son's refusal to be at his father's burial seems to be related with his unfair imprisonment.

As in "Mourning," the structural and stylistic patterns of "Afterwards" are formed by a profusion of symbolic elements which help Benet to build his fiction coherently and expressively. The water around the house and the ringing of the bells are the two most important extended metaphors employed to develop the work. The narrator's assertion that the "waters of time undermine the walls to restore the true balance of chaos" (183) is decisive for the understanding of the pessimistic outlook of the work. The statement not only refers to the fact that time leads man to destruction, but more importantly, to the existential truth that chaos is the very reality from whence man arises and to which man is doomed to revert. Furthermore, man's existence is a disturbing force that must be logically eliminated to "restore the true balance of chaos." Time becomes man's destroying and chaos-restoring force. Artistically, this thematic development is embodied in the recurrent presence of the water which gradually increases as the novelette—man's life— moves onward to destruction: "the water had risen so much that it passed [the tutor's] ankles; the vine's stanchions were rotten and part of the tree was lying dead on the ground." This is the same vine that shaded the window at which the men of the house used to sit to look at the sunset on the mountains (183). The overflow of the water coincides with the son's death. "The garden was covered all over with water. Part of the house was already flooded. It seemed as if the coffin—which was lying in the hallway, because of the water—were about to take off sailing" (206). The other major symbol in "Afterwards" is the obsessive sound of the doorbell. The novella opens and closes with this image of special creative power. The back door of the house, where the bell has been ringing for many years, is finally opened, and a child rushes into the flooded garden and hallway (207). This same symbolic child, who has been ringing the bell the whole time, may be seen as the new beginning which springs out of chaos, the future that is being raised out of the ruins of the past, continuing the cyclical movement of death and rebirth present in the previous works (particularly in "Baalbec, a Stain") and "Mourning." The fusion of these two symbols at the end of the work (specifically in the last paragraph) suggests Benet's deep concern for structural unity and coherence in his fiction. In fact, the fusion is in itself a metaphor, for it becomes the merging point of death and rebirth, and, consistent with the thematic framework, the merging point of the consolidation of the "balance of chaos" and the beginning of its upsetting process. The final descriptive detail, "by the door there was a white rubber ball, the size of an orange, floating on the water" (187), alludes to the same idea through the image of the "white rubber ball [rebirth] floating on the water" (death) which interlocks itself with the fantastic appearance of the child's hand coming out of the water to ring the doorbell, early in the work.

It is enlightening to examine together the main thematic and technical characteristics of *You Will Never Get Anywhere* as a whole, that is, as a work of art in which its parts, although independent from each other, comprise a total structural unity embodying a specific vision of life. The four works underline man's nothingness in time and space. An individual, a family, a generation, or an entire era is rooted in nothingness to bear, in turn, nothingness. This pessimistic cyclical pattern makes of the characters in all these novelettes not so much individuals developed according to traditional tenets of depiction, as symbolic shadows whose *raison d'etre* is subject to the total vision of the work.[3] That is, character is not subjugated to any ideal of realistic consistency, but to the effectiveness of the system of expression. Rather than an end in itself, Benet's personages are merely a means for the enigmatic creation of the novel. The same conviction of artistic independence from the traditional concept of the novel is also perceptible in the author's skillful engineering of plot and handling of time. With the possible exception of the first two novelettes, where "something happens," plot is minimal, almost nonexistent. Events, stripped of their realistic apparel, do not stand for themselves as signs of chronological sequence, but are almost imperceptible references in the midst of the characters' (or the narrators') flow of reflections. The events are there not for the plot's sake, but for the elucidation of the characters' conceptions of the world. The order in which they are arranged is determined by the characters' patterns of reflection rather than by a chronology of occurrence decided by the author, which explains why juxtaposition of past, present, and future is found throughout the collection. The fragmentation of Benet's typically long sentence through repeated subordinate clauses containing past, present, and future becomes the symbolic microcosm of the organic juxtaposition in the plot of the work, which in turn is the composite image of man's labyrinthine existence.

Other important technical modes common in the collection are (1) the use of symbols to infuse a variety of levels of reality and to give structural unity to the work, since these symbols are developed and transformed into extended metaphors; (2) the careful elaboration of mystery, paralleling life's enigma in which characters and readers are trapped and must find their way out through an interpretation of man's destiny; (3) the implementation of irony and absurdity in the character's thoughts and actions, which inevitably lead him to nowhere; and (4) the persistent recurrence of uncertainty regarding the distinction between reality and fantasy, between the natural and the supernatural, as in the case of the flying cups of "Afterwards." Benet's approach to reality, to conventional reality, recalls that of García Márquez, yet there are no grounds for implying influences from the latter upon the former, for this collection appeared six years before Márquez's *One Hundred Years of Solitude*.

A Tomb

Unlike Benet's other novelettes, *A Tomb* (1971) has received a good deal of critical attention and has become one of his most widely read pieces of fiction.[4] This relative "popularity" may be due to the following factors. First, *A Tomb* was never part of a collection, having appeared independently and in the attractive series *Palabra e Imagen* [Word and Image], of Editorial Lumen, which gave the individual work immediate exposure and visibility. Second, compared to *You Will Return to Región* and *A Meditation,* two very long and intricate novels, the short, easy-to-follow text of *A Tomb* immediately satisfied, at least partially, the reader's curiosity regarding Benet's art. Finally, in addition to carrying over some of the technical characteristics of the previous works, especially of *You Will Never Get Anywhere,* which passed unnoticed because the author was unknown when it first appeared, *A Tomb* is Benet's first step into the realm of the ghost story, a genre not too common in Spanish literature, but which Benet would continue to practice in his later and important book *5 Tales and 2 Fables.* It is from this perspective, of the text as a ghost story, that critics have approached the work. I shall use the same perspective, but merely as a point of departure for a different, yet complementary, interpretation.

In *A Tomb* the anonymous child must continue the sinister and evil legend of his great-grandfather, a nineteenth-century Brigadier poisoned by his enemies in retaliation for his perverse actions as a man and as a soldier. The child does not know exactly why or how this must be so, and indeed is unaware of what is happening. The reader does sense, however, that throughout the work some mysterious forces are establishing, as Gullón says, "a tacit pact"[5] between the child and his ancestor, a pact whereby he "will acquire the diabolical powers associated with the house and the Brigadier."[6] But as this sinister connection is being formed, and its mystery unfolds, the child's existence plunges deeper into confusion, loneliness, and insecurity, an insecurity further complicated by the lady's decision to leave the child (left with her by his father) with the caretaker of the Brigadier's tomb.[7]

Even though the preceding interpretation is a valid one, it does not reach far enough into the symbolic structure of the work. It is important to focus on what is actually happening to the child as a result of the sinister connection being established. *A Tomb* reflects a frightening world where life is conceived and experienced by the individual (the child) as being equally as destructive and annihilating as death itself. The two concepts are here metaphysically interchangeable. Man's (or the child's) life is nothing but the verification of the dissolution of his will and of his sense of individuality, with no possibilities for redemption or personal freedom. His life is what the tomb has been keeping inside for him through generations: the annihilation of his personal freedom and the never-ending fermentation of hatred and vengeance. His life has to be what the tomb symbolizes for his family and for the enemies of his family. He is a passive receptor and perpetuator of a family legacy, with no choice but to be what the tomb, the Brigadier's legacy, forces him to be, the defender of the tomb's values. In other fictional works of his, Benet suggests that man's existence is a tomb: in *A Meditation,* the narrator-protagonist states that his grandfather purchased his house when in the area there were only a few ruined peasant families who did not leave the region, not even when impelled by the "urge to abandon their tomb" (8). The protagonist in *A Tomb,* as a passive receptor of hatred and vengeance, finds himself in a situation where his destiny has already been determined by external forces which he can neither comprehend, overcome, nor reject. He is seen as a living death, hanging in a vacuum or buried in a tomb filled with hatred and vengeance, and empty of love and hope. Quite significant is the fact that he is still a child, unable to judge or decide for himself, a passive observer of the destruction of his own being. He *must be* the heir of his ancestor's legend. When forced to move from one home to another for his protection, to avoid the brutal vengeance of his family's enemies, the only thing he can do is sense his own presence as a mere expectation or an awaiting (18). But what is he expecting or awaiting? Either for another possible blow of vengeance about which he knows nothing, and for which he cannot be held responsible, or for a possible relocation, because he was destined to be taken to other places (most likely he will remain in the same place indefinitely). In section I, which is in fact the last one, the omniscient narrator leaves the child waiting indefinitely for that promised relocation (18). His total passivity and impotence (he perhaps cannot even hate) make the reader see him as a nonexistent entity whose sense of individuality has been and continues to be progressively deteriorating in the social tomb in which he was born. The sun, says the narrator, "was glittering as never before in many months and the shadow of the child was cast, from top to toe all along the tomb . . . as a sign of identification and recognition of the place which was reserved for him" (9). His individual deterioration (in the symbolic tomb) progresses as he grows older and becomes more capable of carrying out the "responsibilities" implied in the secret pact with the Brigadier. The Brigadier at one extreme of time (distant past) and the child at another (now) are linked by the tomb-home in which he was born, must live, and for which he must die. The tomb is both the nexus between past and present and the unifying force between Brigadier and child. The unification is so intense that there is only one entity: the Brigadier is the child, and vice versa. The latter is an extension of the former. And it is in this connection or fusion of identities that the core of the mystery lies.

One may say that not only the child but also the guard or caretaker exhibits the same state of passivity, awaiting the retaliation of the Brigadier through the child. (Remember, the child is awaiting, among other things, the time when he will be an active heir of the Brigadier, i.e., will carry out his responsibilities assumed in the secret pact.) Conflicting with this fear, he must continue to take care of the child and the tomb. Tomb and child—of which he is afraid—must be under his care; he does not know why, but "he does it as if he had received an order coming from far away," an order he can neither impugn nor ignore (11). Both child and guard, who are enemies but depend on each other, spend the long years of war sitting at the kitchen table in physical and spiritual immobility, the former resting his head on his arms and the latter, on his hands. (23–24).

The tomb image, used here to express man's metaphysical immobility, suggests other complementary ideas that enhance the significance of the work. Parallel with immobility, there is a dynamic force: time. It perpetuates that immobility and intensifies and evinces man's constant deterioration. Each season further putrefies the individual (7–8). This brings up another consideration: that in the novel there is a timeless vacuum where the protagonist has been cast and also a flux of time that nurtures that vacuum. Besides, the cyclical passing of the seasons (8) and the recurrent reference to the days of the Spanish Civil War are used as contrasting and dynamic background for the portrayal of the individual's immobility. Also, this chronological force is perceptible to the protagonist insofar as it marks the rhythm of his progressive deterioration, i.e., of awaiting the time when he must perform his duties as the Brigadier's active heir. In *A Tomb*, the perception of time comes through the deterioration of one's will and individuality, i.e., through the child's awareness of his responsibility as the Brigadier's heir. Hatred and vengeance, the two main unifying forces in the novel, are not only passed on from generation to generation, but most importantly, they become more intense as time passes (56); so the town and the child's family, with the passing of time, shall become also more and more frantic and fermented enemies of each other. The people's hatred and vengeance reach the proportion of an evil ritual, portrayed in the work via the image of the goats used as mascots or amulets by the mob on its way to the assault of the family's tomb and home (32–52). These episodes take the form of a demonic allegory: the mob fiercely breaks and burns everything it finds; it drinks and fornicates, while from a hidden place the child (innocence) passively witnesses what they do to his family. To heighten the inevitability of the evil forces on the one hand (people) and underscore the deep sense of impotence on the other (child), the author, with a deceptive pretension of realism and suspense, describes—in detail—how they approach the house, what they do to it, and also what the hidden victims say and do about it (nothing).[8] And the mere allusion to the Pacientes road, which the enemies use to reach the house, becomes in the mind of the reader and of the child a symbol of vengeance and impotence. He can only see the presence and action of the mob, but he cannot explain either why they do what he sees or what it all means to him. Only the reader is able to understand it, which, in turn, makes the situation of the character more tragic and painfully ironic, as the reader can see what the child, the real victim, cannot.

The complexity of the novel derives primarily from the enigmatic structure of symbols used to convey the main character's psychological conflicts resulting from his present situation and from the narrator's mode of perceiving reality which, consistent with the character's major problem, is incarnated in a baroque style throughout the novelette. Neither the narrator nor the reader knows exactly who *la señora* ("the lady") taking care of the child actually is. He was left under her custody and she is one of his relatives. His feelings toward her are ambivalent: he sees in her a mother and a lover. In his abandonment he turns instinctively to her for protection (50), but a protection that will not last because she will also be forced to leave him and consequently pass the child to the tutelage of the guard and his wife. So there is in him a growing feeling of insecurity that, coupled with his metaphysical immobility deriving from the secret pact with his ancestor, prevents him from developing a normal sense of individuality. Obviously, he finds in the lady some kind of a mother-lover-protector, whose protection he needs in his present isolation given the lack of mother and father. Also his instinctive curiosity for the tomb and the mystery he senses in it can be taken as a symbolic contradiction, in that he wants to learn the *cause* of his spiritual deterioration at the same time he resorts to the tomb as a *refuge*. What else is left for him, after he has been abandoned by the lady in the hands of his enemy, the caretaker? Naturally, the tomb of his ancestors, the tomb for which he must do what it expects him to do, is also the tomb that gives him an identity, the identity of belonging to the line of the sinister Brigadier.

Consistent with the character's lack of awareness of causes and of what is happening to his being, the narrator's mode of presenting the novelistic world is, at times, limited to the "perhaps" or "almost" formulae that abolish omniscient certainty. He must therefore report the mystery or legend of this family at times with some certainty and at times with uncertainty; his report is subject to how complete or incomplete that legend is found by him after it has been passed among the people, which explains why he knows more about some things than others, why he can be more complete in some cases and less detailed in others, and why he is forced at times to fill some gaps with his own comments.

The plot is not as complicated as that of Benet's major novels and short stories. One can follow and understand what is going on. Any complication in plot development stems from the irregular disposition of the four sections: chronologically, the book should have the following sequence: III, II, IV, I, from past to present; but the narrator disregards it and arranges his material following a different order which serves to rarefy the already mysterious world of the novelette. The same purpose is served by the following devices: (1) the anonymity of the characters except the guard's wife; (2) the physical deterioration of the house and the tomb; (3) the obvious exaggerations used to describe certain events that become almost fantastic, such as the Brigadier's "incredible" resistance to death, reminiscent of Rasputin's, as some critics have observed;[9] (4) the narrator's "intentional" withholding of information; (5) the narrator's habit of never specifying the time when an action takes place; and (6) the black and white photographs scattered throughout the book, making it possible to experience visually the deterioration of the individual, his tomb, and his home.

"Sub Rosa"

"Sub Rosa" is the last composition included in the book of stories by the same title published in 1973.[10] Unlike most short pieces of fiction of the book in question, "Sub Rosa" is a novelette structured around a more or less recognizable plot of considerable length and suspense. The narration is divided into five sections which—with the exception of the first—follow a chronological order and a normal sequence of events leading to the sinking of the *Garry* and the subsequent incrimination, imprisonment, and natural death of its recalcitrant captain, Valentín de Basterra.

In part I, which chronologically should be placed at the end, the reader learns two basic sets of facts: on the one hand, that Basterra has pleaded guilty to the crime,[11] that he has been sent to jail and pardoned, and that before his release he has died of natural causes; and on the other, that he has refused all efforts by his family, friends, and political groups to review his case. What the reader (and apparently the narrator) does not know, however, is what the motives for the crime were. And this is the axis around which the whole structure of the work revolves, the central mystery that will never be revealed in its entirety. In part II, a history of the ship *Garry*, the company to which it belongs, and Basterra's association with the company is given in a quite detailed, traditional, uncomplicated fashion. Part III, the most enigmatic and perhaps the most important of all, introduces a subplot, that of the woman and child living in the small village near Consolación. Basterra visited them before departing to Spain in command of the ill-fated ship whose mission was to take some political prisoners to the mother country. As part of the crew, and as Basterra's second in command, Saint-Izare, a young French-Cuban sailor, was also included. Part IV provides an elaborate, technical account of how the ship survived all the weather complications during the first two weeks on the high seas. In part V, the crew, dissatisfied with Basterra's performance as captain, and realizing that his physical and mental deterioration had seriously hindered already the normal operation of the ship, unanimously decided to replace him with Saint-Izare. Taking this incident as insubordination, Basterra went to the pilot house and, at gunpoint, forced the helmsman to turn back the already damaged ship and killed three persons, including his rival Izare, who was trying to avoid the "tragedy" (261–62).

In looking for the possible motives behind the protagonist's criminal behavior, one must consider first some of the narrator's remarks concerning the enigmatic nature of his story and the inherent certainty that "it [his story] shall always lack truth" (218), "truth as a category that is put off while we live, that dies with what is dead and does not arise again from the past; and since its resurrection is not possible we must always wait for its advent, because truth can neither be a cipher nor a fact nor an abstraction, but rather something that lives and does not manifest itself" (212). This philosophical perception and definition of truth is the central theme of the work and determines its methods of composition. The narrator, stripped of Olympian omniscience, operates on the same level of knowledge about the material he narrates as the reader does, knowing no more or no less than the reader, waiting with the reader for the "advent" of truth. One can sense everywhere how the narrator, tormented by this limitation, would very much like to find out, for instance, what the secret, hidden in Basterra's dialogue with the woman, actually was (235). The narrator, says Ricardo Gullón, "seems to say whatever he knows, but cannot go beyond what he sees and hears."[12] The "advent" of truth—the truth concerning the captain's motives for committing the crime—may come about, perhaps, by manipulating "some details," says the narrator. But what details, the reader must ask, if all of them are either incomplete or as enigmatic as the principal mystery which most characters in the work strive to clarify? For example, the four reports given by the priest, the anonymous drunkard, one of the crew members, and the Cuban ship-builder contradict themselves and further obscure the case (217–18).

Benet's arrangement of the sections is effective and ironic. By including in the first one all the verifiable facts and the information that the motives behind the crime are unknown, he builds the narrative "suspense" for the reader and also for his narrator. The remaining four sections, therefore, constitute an effort on the part of the narrator to find and relate those motives, i.e., in those four sections the suspense increases, seeking the truth as to why Basterra sank the ship. But, in reality, what happens is that the suspense never ends because the motives are never revealed. So the novella concludes where it started: with the same mystery shrouding the motives behind the crime. And the person who laughs at the ignorance of reader, narrator, and everyone else in the tale is Basterra, who dies taking with him the truth of the secret behind his crime.

"Numa"

"Numa" is Benet's latest novella, published as part of his book *Del Pozo y del Numa (un ensayo y una leyenda)* [Of Pozo and Numa (an essay and a legend), 1978].[13] It deals with the mysterious and ubiquitous guard Numa, already in Benet's fiction a legend in his own right. He is charged with watching over the sacred forest, a forest menaced in vain and persistently by an anonymous outsider or intruder. The mystery of both Numa and the intruder, and their instinctive desire to protect and tread upon the forest, is successfully sustained throughout the entire narrative discourse in the same way it is sustained in Benet's other major works. But unlike these works, this "legend" contains a deceptive intention and a special narrative method which the author employs to create—for the first time—a complete and comprehensive account of Numa. The reader is led to believe that this is the opportunity to grasp fully the elusive nature, personality, character, intentions, and intuitions of the legendary Numa. To this purpose Benet incessantly accumulates a variety of information concerning these vital aspects of Numa. The reader learns, for instance, that Numa, in accordance with nature's cyclical changes, has his winter of full rest and his summer of hard work, his autumn of partial rest and his spring of moderate work. The reader also finds out that Numa's mission and authority derive from the "Property," that he has serious inner conflicts and doubts about himself and about his mission (120–21), about his power to continue protecting the forest, and about how the succession to his power must be made. Benet induces the reader to see and feel the human substance of his legend. All the "informative" and "clarifying" material brought forth here, however, is handled in a way that leaves the character in his original state of mystery and the reader, likewise, with his original curiosity, the desire to find out more about Numa. Paradox is the rhetorical device Benet utilizes to play this trick. Numa is neither somber nor joyful (102). He has no character, yet he is stern (123) and totally determined to carry out his duties with utmost dedication and efficiency (102). He does not seem to age (102), yet he worries about his succession when he senses his frailty.[14]

Every bit of information ironically both creates and destroys the objectivity of the legend. This is important to emphasize here because this literary piece, this legend, is supposedly the most thorough and complete portrayal of Numa in Benet's fictional world. And the reader sees that, indeed, it is complete but at the same time, and paradoxically, helps very little to clarify the mystery of the character. The brilliant and persuasive reasonings handled by the objective narrator in the exposition of his material make him appear as a very reliable instrument for the discovery of the inner truth about the two opposing and irreconcilable forces (Numa-intruder) and motivations that make up the legend or history of Numa's domain—or, one may say, of Franco's Spain. One understands the narrator's lucid statements. He says (and it is simple, just like Numa's mind) that he, Numa, knows exactly what his mission is: the protection of the forest. His consolation is that he has this limited function in life, which he needs as it needs him. He knows he is sure what his function is because that is the only thing he knows in life (105–6), and this fact helps him to assert his freedom and his own self. Logic does not help him, however, to understand the reasons for the intruder's persistence in attempting to enter the forest. If Numa were to understand the other's position he would endanger his mission, i.e., his own self. He must remain isolated, neither happy nor sad, wrapped up in his own mystery, blinded by his own obsession, victim of his own simplistic logic. The intruder, on the other hand, must keep trying in vain to enter the forbidden land, knowing that his attempts are futile and that the forbidden forest is an impossible reality to reach (132). He is also victim of his own logic and obsession.

As suggested earlier, this legend is, among other things, an extended metaphor of Franco's Spain. Unlike Benet's other works, here the reference to Spanish historical reality is more subtle. Between the lines, one finds allusions to the traditional conflict between Republicans and Nationalists, allusions to Juan Carlos as the young and timid successor of Franco, allusions to Franco's semidivine right to rule Spain in death as well as in life. This substructure of meaning, of course, does not undermine the universality of the conflict implicit in the narration. Instead it enriches and enhances its ambiguity: it is one thing and also another, both at the same time.

As in Benet's major long works of fiction, in this legend plot is reduced to a minimum, making the narrative an immobile body of discourse. The confrontation at the end, between Numa and the unknown intruder who, more than a real person, seems to be a recalcitrant shadow in Numa's paranoid mind, is the only spark of action in the whole legend. It is not a plot in the traditional sense of the word, but rather an epilogue or appendix, attached to the end in order to show in action the conflict reasoned in the discourse of the text. The intruder seems to die by two shots, one in the buttock and the other in the face. For the reader's momentary relief, or better yet, for his further confusion and exhaustion, Benet resorts—as he does in his other works—to some recurrent symbols: the cloud of dust and the gray lamina of water wherein the two protagonists of history or legend must remain forever. Numa's legend (forest) is as eternal as the change of the seasons or as certain as the intruder's hopes that will turn inevitably into failure.

Benet's use of the third-person narrative point of view is effective. He does not allow Numa or the intruder to speak to the reader or to each other. They are confined to their corners of silence and solitude, there to live, fermenting mutual hatred and hostility, with no hope for communication or possible reconciliation. As they are mysterious to each other, so are they both to the reader and to the narrator. The language Benet uses to build this mysterious legend is consistently technical, cold, and precise. His clauses are extensive and broken in his usual fashion, with parentheses, hyphens, and commas, all contributing to make the text purposely an inflexible, alienating, and exhausting narrative discourse. The textual monotony is even visual, for there is one single paragraph of sixty-nine pages, a technical device used already in *A Meditation*, which is another paragraph, but this time of 329 pages.

Chapter Six

The Short Story:
A Gallery of Enigmas

To the present, Benet has published two major collections of short stories: *5 narraciones y 2 fábulas* [5 Tales and 2 Fables] and *Sub Rosa*, that is, a total of fifteen short stories and two very brief, witty fables. As in the case of the novelettes, these two collections reveal Benet's artistic unity within a narrative variety. Enigma and futility continue to be the central forces of artistic creation and life, in Región or New York, among the young and the old, in situations of love, lust, greed, ambition, or death. Benet's short fiction, including the novelettes, is a gallery of enigmas incarnating passions that cover "a large part of human behavior's complex spectrum."[1]

5 Tales and 2 Fables

5 Tales and 2 Fables, published in 1972, is Benet's first collection of short stories.[2] In addition to the tales and fables, a transcription of four appropriate verses from *The Listeners* by Walter de la Mare and a suggestive drawing for each narrative unit are included.[3] The introductory reference to the English writer evinces Benet's enthusiasm for the former's inspiring and influential fiction, particularly his ghost stories, which have been admired by other contemporary writers.[4] Like de la Mare, who entitled his stories with one or two cryptic words such as "Kismet," "De Mortuis," and "A Mote," Benet, in order to heighten the impact of mystery from the very beginning, does the same with puzzling titles such as "Syllabus," "Catalysis," and "Viator." Furthermore, like de la Mare's "A:B:O," Benet calls one of his stories "TLB." Unlike the narrative units of his novelettes, these tales are briefer and, to some extent, less intricate, but still enigmatic. The ambiguity felt by the readers and characters at the end of each narration is consistently structured with irony and paradox. Man's desires to overcome his fears give rise to an ambivalent situation, for they may or may not be regarded as actually fulfilled; it depends on the reader's stand and mode of arranging the fragments of the magic mosaic, and on the characters' perception of their own schismatic reality. Unlike *You Will Never Get Anywhere,* the characters in the five tales—to rarefy the atmosphere and close certain avenues leading to the understanding of the stories' meaning—are anonymous and limited to one, two, or three per unit.[5] This minimal number makes the story more apt to remain hermetic, since there are fewer perspectives available to the reader for his journey into the heart of fiction. Together with the absence of dialogue, it makes solitude more prominent, even inevitable. Insofar as the fables are concerned, they seem out of place in an otherwise coherent and unified book of fiction. Their inclusion undermines the impact of the five stories as a whole. They constitute a different world both thematically and stylistically, which of course shows the versatile imagination of the author and, on the other hand, may be a justification for their inclusion.[6]

"TLB"

"Until an evening when some knocks on the door, knocks extending for a brief period of time, were heard" is the opening statement (sentence!) of "TLB," the first narration in this collection. It is as if the story, headed by such a statement, were missing a beginning that was told by the narrator before his actual account (the printed story) to the reader, as if the narrator believed that the reader knew exactly whatever came before this statement, and would base the understanding of the work on the reader's perception of the "missing" part. Nothing happens in "TLB": an individual at the local bar dares to bet that he will go and knock on the door of a mill that has been abandoned and forgotten in the minds of the people for almost a century. Once the betting is formalized, he goes there and knocks on the door while his contenders discreetly remain, witnessing his courage, far away from the mill. No one responds to the knock. It is midnight. He tries again, this time with his fist and elbow. Since no one answers, he shouts, hurls a rock at the windows, and, finally, kicks the door. As if he were disappointed, he leaves the place to join the others. When everyone is gone, a voice from the mill answers: "Here we are, come in" (19).

Suspense, the structuring force and main impact of the story, becomes dreadful to the character and the reader alike. The protagonist's act of betting is a subconscious manifestation of his terror of the old mill and of his desire to overcome this fear. It is up to him to prove to himself and to the others his determination and courage. The question as to whether or not the character succeeds in his quest for self-assurance reveals the irony of the situation. At first his knock is "discreet" (13); he is afraid; later, more confident and already convinced that no one is inside, not only does he knock with his fist and elbow, but he aggressively throws rocks at the windows and kicks the door, ignoring, however, the fact that any proof of his courage would turn against himself or would drag him back to his fear, "as soon as he would detect any sign of the presence he needed to offend" (18). This means that, had he still been there to hear the mysterious words coming from inside, "Here we are, come in," all of his efforts might have been in vain. But, since he had already left, convinced no one was inside (and this is his reality), his fear was ostensibly overcome and his courage proven to himself and to his friends. From the reader's point of view, however, this ironically constitutes the character's self-deception, because in order for him truly to conquer his fear he needed to test his courage by facing and experiencing the reality of the mill as it actually is (as perceived by the reader) and not as what it seemed to be (as perceived by the character). However plausible this interpretation may seem, it raises more questions than it answers. Could it not be that his aggressiveness (he throws rocks at the windows and kicks the door before he leaves) may also be a sign of anger at being unable to test and prove his courage (to himself) since no one or nothing emerged to confront him? Could it be, then, that he is cognizant of the failure of his intent, even though his friends may think the opposite?

The complexity of the story's formal disposition is the embodiment and enhancement of the mystery of its content. As the opening words had their input in the formation of mystery, so have the closing ones. By concluding the story with "Here we are, come in," the narrator forces the reader, rather than the intruder, to experience visually and audibly the mill's reality (or fantasy?). It is as if the latter's insistence upon disturbing the solitude and silence of the tomblike building were to be paid for by the former. The circularity of the narration, built with the two statements, makes the reader's confinement in mystery an inescapable experience. It seems as if he were captured and imprisoned in the mill or the story while the intruder escaped. He was led and left inside with no possible exit.

There are many rarefying elements in the story; at first they seem
to be insignificant details, but, as in a poem, they are crucial to
the total effect. The time when the action occurs, twelve o'clock at
night; the fearsome location of the mill near the old tower in the
middle of a thick grove; the total anonymity of the participants;
the insistent repetition of the words, "Is anyone home?," answered
by a dusky silence which permeates the dilapidated house; and the
brevity of the story itself intensify the impact of fear and suspense.

"Reichenau"

"Reichenau" has a dual structure corresponding to the protagonist's antithetical experiences. In part one,[7] the anonymous protagonist—a peddler of "goods which at that time were not of prime
necessity" (31)—finds himself lost at a crossroads in the thick of
the night and in the middle of nowhere. On his way to Región, he
decides to spend the night at an inn. The innkeeper shows him to
his room, informing him that if he needs anything he should simply
ring the bell and help will come right away (26). He falls asleep
almost instantly, but not for long, since at an indefinite time af-
terward strange female voices awaken him. As he switches on the
light, the voices cease, resuming again when he turns it off. His
fear heightens as the voices move closer and closer, and he suddenly
discovers that the lightbulb has burned out. He wants to ring the
bell but decides against it, feeling that this act would be humiliating
to his ego. It is contrary to his pride to have to depend on someone
else for such protection (30); the innkeeper's leer of superiority
revealed at the moment he offered his help is remembered by the
protagonist and later becomes his source of strength. In the second
part, the peddler has become a prosperous businessman, staying at
the Reichenau Hotel for the night, not far from Lake Constanza.
Here he is tormented again by the same female voices, but this time
he rings the bell, asking for help. The concierge's apparent enjoyment and delight derive from the protagonist's fear of the mysterious
noises and the total collapse of his pride and self-sufficiency (34).
The story becomes an unusual battle of egos. On one side the
protagonist at first wins and later loses; on the other, the concierge
at first loses and later wins. Vengeance is the primary motive. The
former thinks that by not using the bell he was affirming his ego
and negating that of the innkeeper; the latter, on the contrary,

knows that it was only a mistaken attitude, causing the protagonist's final downfall. He realizes, as does the reader, that if he were to have rung the bell, he would have avoided the unnecessary complications of the first night and the embarrassment of the second.

The female voices may be viewed as his subconscious fears and desires to affirm his own self or personality. The question here, as in "TLB," is whether or not, when he resorts to the bell at the end, the protagonist succeeds in achieving a balance in his personality. Did he "surrender" (33), as the narrator seems to believe he did? Or, rather, is this so-called surrender a redeeming act for his own self or personality, since what he did was simply to renounce his former mistaken attitude toward the innkeeper's presumptive hostility? Again, the reader has been led into a state of ambiguity that inevitably undermines the absolute nature of any one interpretation. The first act may constitute either a heroic or a ridiculous manifestation of the character's ego. The second one may be regarded in the same manner: as a sign of weakness and surrender or one of maturity and self-confidence. It is as if the author forced the reader's attention to be focused not on the facts as such, but on their mutual relationship, which is never clearly revealed or easily detected.

"Syllabus"

"Syllabus" is the story of a well-known retired historian, Professor Canals, who is invited by a private college to conduct a series of lectures. He finds this opportunity to be delightful and also necessary to test his findings and advance in his research. Those selected for the course are very few in number and are highly qualified. The professors' and students' expectations concerning this new experience are high. Shortly before the first scheduled lecture, Canals receives an unexpected letter from a mysterious individual interested in taking the course. Moved by the letter's honesty and frankness, and despite previous rejections of many qualified students and the fact that the class was to be small, he is not only willing to accept him, but also to register for him and pay all his necessary fees. The absurdity of Canals's kindness and diligence in helping this individual is that it will complicate his teaching and his life as well. At first, the professor is puzzled by this student's sporadic attendance and methodic indifference toward his teaching and ideas. In vain he devises ways to attract his attention and stimulate his interest, but the harder he tries, the more he fails, for the student's conviction of the professor's superficiality increases in proportion as the latter is more willing to share his knowledge. The story culminates with Canals's total collapse before his class, both as an educator and as an individual. Here, the reader will again notice Benet's ability to play with his characters' uncertainties. It is a gradual and painful self-discovery that the professor undergoes. Moved by the honesty of the letter, he accepts the participation of the force which will unveil his superficiality and help to define his true self. His lectures—his creations (51)—can no longer be patterned and developed according to his previous practice and false outlook of history, but according to the exigencies of the mysterious individual, who becomes, in a sense, the symbol of truth and honesty embodied in the spirit of his letter (41). The professor realizes the falseness of his present view of history and also intuits that of his opponent. But is he willing to give up the former for the latter? If so, does he try and succeed? The reader cannot come up with definite answers but should grasp and admire the professor's eagerness to accept the potential challenge foreseen in the letter. It is only by accepting it that he found his new identity, even though it meant embarrassment and self-inflicted pain. If this is true, then what was previously thought to be his total collapse as an educator and an individual is a symbol of his new identity. Now, he knows he is not what everyone thought him to be—the great intellectual and true researcher—but merely a man of limited scope and capabilities. The death of his former deceptive identity gives rise to his new one.

As in the other two stories, here man's self-discovery is not a planned but an unexpected occurrence. The reader's experience is the reflection of the characters' experience, permeated by difficulties, ambiguities, and relativities. They are never quite sure of the significance of their hopes and actions geared toward the elucidation of their selves. It is important to note that the protagonist is a historian whose mania was to see the bitter chain of abuses and tragedies which constitute the essence of history (and of his lectures) as a sequence of *tolerable* events (50–51). The discovery of his new self involves, then, the discovery of a new perception of history, the realization of history as a sequence of *intolerable* abuses and tragedies. To use the author's experience in explaining a work may be inappropriate and misleading, but knowing Benet's persistent criticism against his educators, one is inclined to see the author through the anonymous individual, who not only unmasks the professor but also reveals the macabre face of history, specifically of Spanish history, which, as one of the characters in *You Will Return To Región* puts it, was identified as a sequence of "turmoil and fermented bitterness" (180).

"Catalysis"

"Catalysis" is another of Benet's enigmatic and challenging stories where nothing happens and everything happens. Basically it is about an old couple strolling down a road on a "magnificent" autumn afternoon and a middle-aged man with a dog whom they encounter (65). They seem to be out to marvel at and enjoy the clear blue sky and the landscape's changing colors. The narrator at this point seems to be engaged—with linguistic appropriateness—in the creation of a daily activity with no pretension of ambiguity whatsoever. His realistic posture is such that the reader for a moment is led to believe that the rest of the story is free of Benet's usual conglomeration of obstacles. This is only an illusion, however, one of the several developed in "Catalysis." The story begins to elude the reader's control when the couple suddenly decides to reach the inn where they had once gone before by car, which is located a kilometer ahead, just beyond a curve. On the way, they encounter the man with the dog on three different occasions. As the story slips away from the reader, so does reality from the characters, for they cannot relate the triple presence of the man with the dog with the non-appearance of the inn, noticed by the couple when they reached the curve and could not see the inn which they knew had to be there (just beyond the curve). The questions that readers (and characters) will ask are: Did they actually walk all the way to the inn? Could it be they walked and walked, thinking that they were heading toward the inn when indeed they were not, and that this is why they saw the man with the dog three times? Could it be that the presence of the man with the dog, as well as their own certainty about their getting to the curve, may have been an illusion? All these questions, of course, reveal and underscore the logic of the inquiry the reader is eager to undertake. But the approach is defeating, for those questions can never be answered. If one is to treat the work as a poetic experience, however, where reality and illusion (fantasy) are manipulated on the same level of expression, one will understand and feel not only the author's linguistic ability smoothly to carry on his narrative discourse as if nothing unusual happened on the way, but also the inner artistic harmony of the literary object.

"Catalysis" is a paradoxical illusion, a magic experience where nothing happens and everything happens, where mobility and stability coexist. The characters reach the curve (or it seems that they have) but cannot tell whether they have or not. The man with the dog, as the narrator states, can be seen by the couple "very far away, even though he just passed them" (67). The tension between what is (or seems to be) and what is not (or seems not to be) is the main structural pattern and effect of the story. It permeates the characters' personalities. They enjoy "the peace" of the small village, particularly between summers, but in their inner selves also hate it for they feel isolated, with no other hope but death (50); they miss the city but are inhibited about letting anyone know their true feelings (60).

Perhaps this inner tension or psychological instability plus the impact of the "lightning" they seem to have heard and seen (they are not sure what it was or how it was detected) may have undermined their perception of reality. And, as the narrator says, "the last vestiges of their perception did not help them to take notice that [the man] with the dog, used a walking stick that was almost still and always ahead of his stiff and fast steps" (69). This quotation—from the last paragraph of the story—has an additional function besides proving the deterioration of the characters' perception. It provides some clues leading to the identification of the man with the dog: he is a blind man wearing dark glasses (last two lines) and guided by a dog and a stick (69); it is quite ironic that a blind man should be the one to upset not only their "perception" but their lives as well. When they are petrified to see him again (the last time), they remained still, holding each other's hands and looking open-mouthed at the road ahead, not moving a muscle (69). This sculptural image tells the reader how frightening it was for them to see him again, to perceive, paradoxically, the reality of the man whose mere presence is still undermining their perception. One may say that the man is the catalyst for the reaction to take place in the couple's and the reader's perception of reality.

"Viator"

The importance of this narration lies primarily in its unique structural development and treatment of point of view. Action, as a succession of events, does not exist or is kept to a minimum: the waiting of the protagonist-narrator for the arrival of the train at Cabezas. Instead, the reader's attention is focused upon the three characters' verbal action which defines the structure and rhythm of the composition and the complexity of their embattled existence. The reporter—who later becomes the narrator-protagonist—using an entirely informational, simple style, persistently warns the reader, or anyone interested in going to Región by train, about the problems and afflictions he is destined to undergo: long hours waiting for the train; the encounter with the stationmaster, who does not believe in what he says to those who ask him about schedules; and having to be with someone in the same compartment or waiting room, especially if he is inclined to talk or play cards. The source of the reporter's information is not his experience but people's comments passed on from one generation to another (73–76). He is not part of his report and his objectivity is prevalent: "they say" (74) and "there are some who assert that" (76) are his commonly used introductory words. Part II (77–91) is the central fictional unit, fusing several levels of reality: (1) Here the reporter becomes the protagonist of his own creation and the victim of his own warnings; that is, his reporting turns out to be his reality via its fictionalization. (2) The inveterate talker and card player—whom the protagonist met in the station's waiting room—by talking or informing the latter all about the stationmaster's unique personality, creates another report, another potential reality, to be materialized later with the presence and action of the stationmaster. (3) The stationmaster, in turn, informing the protagonist and the card player about a former stationmaster, creates yet another potential reality to be materialized later with that of his own. What he says about his former co-worker is what people say about himself. The title is ambivalent; on the one hand it is ironically deceiving, for there is no actual traveling in the story, and, on the other, it is symbolically meaningful, for there is a constant shift of perspective on the part of the reader: from a reported potential reality to a proper reality by its respective fictionalization. This dynamic force not only unifies the story but marks its rhythmic pattern as well.

The stationmaster, after alluding to his colleague's highly regarded reputation, reports on the mysterious explosion which takes place at Cornill every 3 November, the same date on which he is reporting. To date, voices on the telephone have always been the prelude to the accident. The questions which arise are: Will this part of the report, the explosion, become a reality? The phone calls have already been made. Will the protagonist still board the potentially suicidal train arriving at Cabezas at 3:50 A.M.? Since every report throughout the story has become a reality, a reality experienced by the characters, will the one concerning the explosion also materialize? It being impossible to answer these questions, the reader is of course left with the protagonist in a state of dreadful uncertainty and panic.

All these unanswered questions emanating from the stories, evince, on the one hand, Benet's regard for fiction as an intellectually entertaining experience and, on the other, a profound modern conviction of reality as a relative concept that precludes any absolute judgment. The uncertainties his characters undergo have a repercussion on the formal composition of the story, essentially mysterious, and the reader's comprehension, meaningfully relative. As one critic has said, understanding Benet's fiction is only an approximation, never an exclusive and absolute interpretation.[8]

The Fables

The fables are brief, witty, and entertaining narratives in which the author displays sharp imagination and linguistic ability to create amenable situations. This is particularly true as regards the second one, in which a jealous husband, a faithful wife, and an innocent friend decide to disguise themselves—without the others' knowledge—in each other's clothes so that they may witness what each other's real conduct is in relation to the husband's real suspicion of his wife's presumptive infidelity with his friend. The main effect of the fable's linguistic manipulation is to make the reader feel lost and totally confused in the most logical and clear situation one can possibly find. Every sentence, precisely because of its clarity and logic, constitutes a step forward toward further confusion. The author's whimsical humor and pleasure in creating sharp and striking situations are obvious.

Sub Rosa

Only a year after the appearance of *5 Tales and 2 Fables,* a new, larger, and more ambitious collection of short stories was published under the title of *Sub Rosa* (1973). It contains nine stories and a novelette bearing the same title as the book.[9] Unlike the two previous collections whose novelettes and stories by and large take place in the mythical Región and its surroundings, and have as a common theme the mental, moral, and physical deterioration and isolation of the individual, *Sub Rosa* depicts a refreshingly diversified, fictional world where Benet exhibits his broad and incisive narrative versatility. Out of the ten compositions of the book, only three take place in, or have anything to do at all with, Región: "Horas en apariencia vacías" [Seemingly Empty Hours], "De lejos" [From Far Away], and "Una línea incompleta" [An Incomplete Line]. This departure from Región, in addition to exhibiting Benet's versatility in the art of fiction writing, as indicated earlier, adds a new dimension to his entire fiction: man is seen in a different vital milieu and perceived from a different perspective. But wherever Benet's characters go they will always be the same losers, the same victims of passions and witnesses of deterioration. In other words, they typically follow the familiar patterns, acting under different circumstances and motives but inevitably ending in the same painful, existentialist way they normally do in Región.

Unlike, for example, the monostylistic collection *You Will Never Get Anywhere*, *Sub Rosa* is a symphonic narrative animated by the same theme and developed with variants of form and execution. Each story has its own technical construction, and most of them offer a unique structural and stylistic configuration that in itself is a novelty within Benet's fictional world. His great narrative talent moves in many directions. It goes from the pure and seemingly simple dialogue of "Obiter Dictum" to the intricate and tedious discourse of "Seemingly Empty Hours," from the uncomplicated narrative point of view of "Garet" to the capricious but effective proliferation of narrative units and points of view in "From Far Away." Mystery is the core of each composition, as it is in all Benet's fiction. There is mystery in the very identity of a person, like the lady who ruins the sexual drives of the man in "Por los suelos" [It Was Ruined]—wherein the reader does not know with certainty if she is his wife or not. There is mystery in what happens to the characters (it is not clear how Durán's father really died in "Así era entonces" [The Way It Used to Be]), mystery in the motives behind an action (Why did Agueda ask her ex-husband to come in "El diablo de la paridad" [The Evil of Parity]?), mystery in what is and what is not real, etc. Not even the narrator himself knows the reality and truth of all that he relates. He knows no more and no less than the reader does and uses the narrative process (as the reader uses the reading experience) as a method of knowledge, knowledge of truth that is never discovered, for truth is—as one narrator puts it—"a category that is put off while one lives" (212). The only truth about the discovery of truth is that such a discovery is a metaphysical impossibility. The author himself as the master of his own poetic creation, one suspects, feels the moral and aesthetic urge to leave his characters wandering in their own mystery, struggling in vain to reach and understand the hidden light that illumines their shadowy existence.

The narrators become at times the puppets the author enjoys playing with, stripping them of their conventional omniscience and making them fail to perform as reliable sources of information of the narrative material. They either contradict themselves or simply volunteer self-incriminatory confessions which reveal their naiveté or profound stupidity about their own existence and that of others. This is the case of "From Far Away" and "The Way It Used to Be." Irony becomes, in all the stories, the most widely used stylistic and rhetorical device. The spirit of the text normally runs in two antithetical directions, toward its assertion and its negation, toward the consolidation of reality and its dissolution, leading, in turn, to the metaphysical impossibility of determining where one ends and the other begins. All the characters strive for power, and power strikes them mercilessly. It is a cruel world where whatever the individual does is that which eventually will undo him. As in most of Benet's other works, in the majority of the stories of *Sub Rosa* action, time, and even space have vanished as conventional novelistic components. The stories are motionless experiences suspended in limbo, captured by a dynamic linguistic force that opens itself in as many directions as there are emotions and thoughts forming the experience. It is this harmonic unification of an immobile, uneventful, and actionless state of being or experience, and a linguistic dynamic force to capture it, that make the reading of Benet's fiction a challenging, demanding, and rewarding adventure.

As in the two previous collections, so also in *Sub Rosa* are greed, lust, and death the trilogy that shapes most of these characters' destiny. Greed and lust propel them to power but also to death. [10]

"Garet"

"Garet," the first tale in *Sub Rosa,* is an entertaining and ironic short story about an anonymous Spanish business representative who has come to New York City to sign some contracts. On a Saturday morning, while tying his shoe near the Frick Museum, he is approached by a chauffeur who asks him if he is waiting for Miss Devenaut, Garet Devenaut. Impulsively he says yes, and the chauffeur proceeds to give him the rest of the message: Garet will not spend the weekend with him due to other pressing matters, but he should go to her parents' home, in Mamaroneck, for the weekend; Garet will call him on Monday. Considering that he does not have much money, that he is alone in the city, and that he has nothing better to do, he decides to continue to act as if the message were indeed for him. So he follows the chauffeur to the limousine, gets in, makes himself comfortable, and, when ready to depart, he sees a man wearing a coat who seems to be waiting for someone. He believes that man is Miss Devenaut's lover. Once at her house, he is bored by the triviality and monotony of the two men and the three women he meets there. Ironically the only thing he likes is the broiler in the house. On Sunday afternoon, he returns to New York City with Augusta, one of the three women at the house, apparently Garet's friend. While with her in his hotel room in New York, he receives a call from Garet, who has obtained from Mark, her brother, the information concerning the place where the protagonist was staying. As the phone conversation continues, he begins to forge an image of her (her age, her clothes, etc.) and to perfect his acting as Garet's real man, and says on the phone that he wants to see her, which she fortunately refuses. His interest is, of course, Augusta, not Garet. As he is being taken from the hotel by his American business associates (so that he may sign the contracts and fly back to Madrid), a pretty young woman arrives at the hotel looking for someone. They see each other in the revolving door as he is leaving and she is coming in. Fascinated by her presence, he believes that if he had seen her moments earlier, before they forced him away, a change in his life might have occurred.

The mystery of the story and its artistic effect derive from the following considerations:

1. Neither the reader nor the anonymous protagonist knows with certainty who the young lady is. Is it Garet, as the protagonist believes, or somebody else who, by mere coincidence, has come to

the hotel to meet someone? The irony is that, as he played on others with his identity, now she plays on him with hers.

2. The story's entire plot emerges from, is activated by, and is led to its conclusion by chance. The protagonist recognizes the influence of fate in man's actions. To this effect, says the narrator upon seeing the man who seemed to be waiting for Garet, "Nothing is more comforting than the correct redistribution that chance imposes, once in a while, on the fortuitous hours" of people (13). This is true since his whole experience in New York and Mamaroneck took its present form through chance. He, and no one else, happened to be present at the right moment and the right place to receive the message from the chauffeur. Also, in the end, his departure and the way it was effected prevented him from meeting the young girl who happened to arrive a bit late.

3. Neither the reader nor the protagonist knows who the man wearing the coat, who "seemed" to be Garet's lover, really was. Notice that he was also affected by the forces of chance because if he had arrived earlier he would have gotten the message, instead of the stranger who becomes the protagonist of the story by mere chance. Chance not only marks the character's course of action, but also fashions his world, the fictional world of the story. If the man wearing the coat had been there sooner he could have been the protagonist, and his story inevitably would have been different. This illusion is one of the main forces that endows the story with mystery and aesthetic charm.

4. The suspense, which runs throughout the entire narration, rests on the protagonist's skill in acting as Garet's man and on the inability of the others to detect his false pretense. The suspense lasts, therefore, as long as his deception runs undetected.

5. At the end, however, he is the victim of his own little game, for it is he who, feeling the special fascination for the young girl (who he thinks is Garet), is unable to meet her, or to forge a meaningful relationship and possibly secure the opportunity—as he himself points out—to change the direction of his life.

"It Was Ruined"

"It Was Ruined" is a brief and seemingly frivolous narration developed through a fragmented and capricious manipulation of reality. In order to deal with the story's structural composition more effectively, we shall divide it into two main sets of events which are interrelated by the protagonist's own complications. In the first part, a young liberated girl has come to a man's (the protagonist's) apartment to make love. At the moment of climax, another woman arrives and the copulation is ruined, hence the title of the story. Unsuspected happenings often ruin the character's plans. At this point in the story everything remains a mystery. The reader is dealing with three anonymous characters. The most the narrator does to identify the people is to indicate that the young girl's name is a common one, as common as, for example, Manola or Paloma or Paz (36). It is uncertain if the protagonist is married or single, if the arriving lady is his wife or another mistress, if the young girl in bed is a casual woman in his life or a professed or undeclared prostitute. What is clear is that she is an independent individual who acts quite maturely and is not a threat to his freedom.

The second part takes place in a whorehouse where the protagonist is seen in a room, again, with a young girl who also leaves when they hear some familiar steps heading to the room where they are undressed. Are those steps his wife's? The arriving lady asks him, "What are you doing there naked?" "What are you doing on the floor?" "Why don't you get up and get dressed?" These are the same questions the madame of the brothel had asked him immediately before the arriving lady did (44). In order to increase the confusion of reality, Benet resorts to a variety of details common to both sets of events (in the apartment and the brothel), such as the familiar noise coming from the front door and the steps in the hallway.

Benet skillfully manipulates reality, and the reader bears the task of determining what is and is not real. The reader does not have to solve the mystery, however, since the narrator himself does not know how. The fictional world in the story poses as a total enigma, with whose parts one can play when trying to put them together. The following are only variants of this game of fiction.

1. The protagonist's experience in his bedroom is a "reality." His wife's arrival hindered his copulation with the young girl. We say it is his wife because she appears in the second part when he is found under similar circumstances. Furious, his wife throws away and destroys what she finds in the bedroom and later abandons him. To him this is not a problem but, indeed, a blessing. He says that since it is not a great loss he will not call her. What bothers him

the most, however, is the fact that he does not know where his young girl might be now (42).

2. The experience in the brothel is an "enigma." Is it only an hallucination occurring in his mind? Yes. The narrator indirectly leads the reader to this interpretation when, at one point, he states that the protagonist was seized by an hallucination that prevented him from realizing when and how the young girl had left him upon hearing the arrival of his wife (44).

This interpretation of the second part, seen as an hallucination, is further reinforced by the "transformation" (that takes place in his paranoid mind) of the madame's questions, directed to him, into those of his wife, also directed to him. The woman he is (or imagines himself to be) in bed with is a young girl, just like the first woman in his apartment. So what seems to be occurring in the brothel is actually occurring in his mind as a repetition of the reality that took place in the apartment. The fact that it occurs in his mind does not make it less real.

3. Although the text permits this interpretation, it also allows the reader to see the set of events in the brothel as an objective reality that actually took place. Benet's texts, one must remember, have this poetic malleability and flexibility. They are not static but dynamic dictions of artistic ambivalence and ambiguity. If indeed the second part is a solid reality, problems of interpretation further proliferate because now one must determine whether such an experience, i.e., that of the brothel, occurred before or after the experience in the apartment. If it occurred before, then the first part of the narration (the experience in the apartment) becomes an hallucination, patterned in details and intensity after the reality of the brothel. And if it occurred after, then part I and part II (the experience in the apartment and the brothel) are realities developed under the similar mysterious and hallucinatory appearance, veiling the consistency of reality which seems to be concurrently one thing and its opposite. That is, the two experiences are simultaneously hallucination and reality. They can be defined neither as pure hallucination alone nor as pure reality.

4. The last possible interpretation is that the two experiences are hallucinated repetitions patterned after a reality that might have taken place in the past or patterned for a reality that the protagonist fantasizes may happen in the future. Benet has immersed the reader into the mainstream of the protagonist's inner conflicts, conflicts

which upset his emotional balance. The reader witnesses the process and outcome of the protagonist's emotional disintegration in the sexual comedy wherein he is both master and victim, the designer of his own trap.

"The Way It Used to Be"

In "The Way It Used to Be," Benet unfolds, through one of his characters, the *innocent* experiences of a young group of bathers that, in the distant past, looking for refuge and fun, used to frequent their unspoiled beaches every summer. The story is told by an anonymous and sentimental member of the group. And the mood and mode of his personal account of what happened during those distant summers that the group spent together are at times naive, sometimes forcefully ironic, and almost always nostalgic. This variety of feeling and consequent variety of expression, prevalent in the reconstruction of the past, endows the narrative with complexity.

By mid-summer, the men of the group became bored and restless because the girls accompanying them did not react favorably to their sexual suggestions and impulses. The boredom, however, suddenly developed into excitement when one of them "discovered" near the sea a nineteen-year-old peasant girl, La Martina, who, we are told, had lived all her life under the control and protection of her father, one of the three innkeepers of the area. Her mysterious and occult presence, plus the natural and radiant beauty and charm she projected, intrigued the young men. So the following summer, led by C. Durán, and using special pretexts and stratagems, they began (literally and metaphorically) to draw her out of her pristine state of innocence, later to cast her into her present ignominious existence. Abruptly abandoned by her disloyal and villainous lover, C. Durán, (who used to allow his friends secretly to enjoy watching her body, that is, without her knowledge), she married Eduardo, one of Durán's close associates who now "does not live well thanks to his refreshment business which he opens in the summer for the numerous bathers, even though it seems that all the weight of his business rests on his wife" (59).

The story has two fundamental mysteries to be considered: (1) Why did Durán suddenly abandon Martina? (2) Do the last lines of the story, quoted above, suggest that Eduardo's wife has become a loose woman, satiating not only the thirst, but also the lust of the bathers, which is why the weight of the business rests entirely on her? Concerning the first question, the reader knows that Durán left the inn (not the inn of Martina's father), where he was taking a siesta with her, and rushed home to do something about his dying father. His father was "a relatively young man," who showed no signs of illness that would justify his premature death (59). So why was he dying? Did La Martina's father kill him in retaliation to what Durán had been doing to his daughter? Yes. And the textual evidence is the following: First, the person delivering the message, a possible witness of the two fathers' fatal encounter, knew exactly where to find Durán. He came directly to the inn where he was taking a siesta with La Martina. Second, purposely, Benet allows no one—except Durán himself—to hear the details of the message. Third, when Durán is leaving the place, he says to the innkeeper "some incomprehensible words," something that "sounded humiliating" (58). The irony of these two evidences is that it is precisely the omission of information that helps to solve the enigma, i.e., one mystery is clarified by another mystery. Fourth, the narrator, in the present, reflecting on the repercussions of these past events, as if suspecting who caused the death of Durán's father, furiously unleashes a series of insults at La Martina's father. The latter is termed a merciless, "worthless" ogre, "a container of filth whose fetidity I will be able to tell even when immersed in the most tattered and ammoniacal dunghill" (52).

Why such a reaction? Because he sees in La Martina's father the one responsible for ruining all those youthful summers when the groups used to go together, before the tragic incident which broke it apart.[11] His shallow mentality does not permit him to perceive the permanent damage the group inflicted upon this unoffensive family of fishermen. To answer the second question, concerning the present situation of La Martina, one must delve into the spirit of the last lines of the story. It seems certain that she is, in fact, a loose woman who satisfies not only the thirst but also the lust of clients. She is now what the group, intentionally or unintentionally, induced her to become ever since they discovered her and pulled her out of the sea. From her initial state of innocence, as a young peasant girl under the loving control of her father, the reader sees her emerging and becoming a debased woman, now working under the control of her husband, Eduardo, the very man who once helped to pull her out of her original purity.

Benet's other critical point, besides the relentless manipulation of his characters in an effort to reveal their frivolous mind and existence, is that those children from good families, just for fun, destroyed the happiness of an inoffensive family of fishermen, who saw in the sea not a seasonal pleasure but a source of daily living. The conflict between the forces of civilization or reason and those of nature or instinct, and the subsequent destruction of the latter by the former, is the ultimate thrust of this narrative.

The story's artistic elaboration offers interesting aspects to be considered. Irony is one of its main ingredients. Benet plays with his narrator—and for that matter with many of the characters—to the extent that his (the narrator's) judgment becomes questionable and his performance as a reliable narrator defective. His romantic and nostalgic recollection of what happened in those summers of his youth does not cause him to reflect on, let alone to repent of, what he and his peers had done to La Martina and her father, but rather to enjoy again the "mischievous" behavior of the group. To the narrator the recollection is, of course, a source of a naive pleasure, but to the reader and the author, the narrator's recollection is inadvertently and ironically a self-incriminating confession whereby all his insults cast at La Martina's father revert to himself and his friends. The other victim of the same irony is of course Eduardo. As one of La Martina's secret admirers and actual witness of her initial sexual relations with Durán, he ends up marrying her and making of himself again a witness, but now a witness of the final phase of her moral deterioration. All this, one must remember, is recollected and told by a naive narrator who misses the very essence and meaning of his own words.

"Seemingly Empty Hours"

Unlike the three previous short stories of *Sub Rosa*, "Seemingly Empty Hours" is a typical Benet text that, stripped of the structural and formal pattern of a short story, takes the form of a long, uninterrupted, narrative discourse which, in view of its stylistic elaboration and theme, may very well be considered as another chapter of the author's major novels dealing with his mythical Región. This means that texts such as this one expand the fictional world of Región, but do not necessarily add anything new and truly significant to what the reader already knows about, and expects from,

Región and its living shadows. Thematically and stylistically, then, this text in relation to Benet's total fiction is—as are a few other similar tales—mere repetition. But as an independent text, "Seemingly Empty Hours" has its own artistic value.

Basically in the tale there are three characters: a captain of the Nationalist army, his aunt, and her servant. After his mission has been accomplished in the battlefield, through merit competition he is assigned a new post as a military judge in Región (a preferred-destination city which he managed to get through special contacts). He wanted to live at his aunt's house to keep her company and help to overcome her recent tragedy, the loss of her husband and her two sons in the Spanish Civil War. His good intentions and altruistic urge, however, do not match with the uncomfortable, chilling indifference of his aunt, who would rather be left alone than be accompanied and consoled by him, a military official, a symbol and a reminder of her tragedy. When he asks her for details regarding their death, the answer is silence and a piercing look of accusation because he is alive and her three men are dead. Whichever side he represents in the Spanish Civil War (Republicans or Nationalists) does not matter to her. He is a military man and, as such, her tacit enemy. Her three men fought for the winning Nationalist cause, yet its victory, since they are dead, is only a "tasteless fruit," a constant reminder of her misfortune and ensuing solitude (76). She also subconsciously sees in him her men; this is the reason why in the midst of her grief and hatred she knits him a woolen sweater to keep him warm and protected.[12]

Communication is nonexistent. Once, she requested him to do something special for her. Since he did not hear her because at that moment he was reading the newspaper, he asked her to repeat it. But, again, only silence and the usual piercing look were offered in return. Later, the captain and the reader learn from the servant that what the aunt had requested was that he find the way to free a prisoner; a twenty-two-year-old nephew awaiting trial in Marceta. Days later, without the reader's direct knowledge, the lady had also asked him to free another relative of hers, a sixty-year-old brother-in-law. The captain willingly proceeds to help her, not only to prove to her that he can be useful but also to cheer her up and, for his own pleasure, to test his power and influence. Unfortunately, though, he only *partially* succeeds with the twenty-two-year-old, and not at all with the sixty-year-old relative. The boy was released but later had to join the army, while the other man had to remain in prison and be executed. All this of course was a blow to his ego and pride and to his incipient relation with his aunt, who must by now distrust him completely. Furthermore, he took all this as a defeat that plunged him into the same state of alienation and frustration as his aunt's. His official victory in the battlefield became, in the long run, a personal defeat in his private life, for he could not save the life of a distant relative (the sixty-year-old man) or provide a minimum of happiness to a closer one, as he had planned to do when he came to live with his aunt. Both are left to endure a life of impotence and hatred since they can do nothing about the damage inflicted on their relatives and on each other. They know now that personal reasons and needs must come after those of the state and, in this case, of the Nationalist cause, an ideal for which they must continue to sacrifice themselves (89).

"From Far Away"

"From Far Away" is a mysterious, technically intricate and rich story told in the first person by two different narrators. The plot is, or seems to be, the following (one cannot be sure about some events). The second narrator himself is not sure either of the content or development. And what is more ironic is that he cannot understand the nature of his own experience, and yet he is anxious to relate it in order to clarify other people's minds and conflicts. [13]

In an after-dinner chat, a family—parents and children—and some friends (the two narrators are among them) engage in a long, tedious discussion of the generation gap, of the children's right to decide for themselves and the parents' responsibilities toward them. The discussion would never have come to an end if one of the most lucid—and paradoxically most confused—of the friends had not tactfully intervened. His intervention, however, is perplexing. First he condemns the parents' urge to dissuade their children from acting according to their own ideas, preferring that they adopt and follow as a guide their parents' experiences (95). This means he favors parents letting their children decide for themselves. Second, he shows how such an alternative, the one he advocates, is only an illusion leading nowhere. And he shows this by telling the reader, and the people at the table, what his experiences were when he left home and joined the working forces of Conrad Blear, a mysterious businessman who also happened to be another failure despite his inevitable reputation of being an intelligent, independent, and rich bachelor. Of course, the enigma here presents several aspects to be considered before an attempt is made to solve it. If the narrator says that children should have the exclusive right to decide for themselves and later shows, through his own experience, how this choice led him nowhere, then how does one react to this absurdity? The reader as well as those at the table were convinced that his story was going to prove the validity of his conviction about children's rights since he advocated it before he even began telling his experience. What did it prove? The opposite of what he advocated? So, is he actually favoring parents' intervention or interference in their children's final choice of their future? No. He is clear and sure about his opposition to this idea. The ultimate thrust of his personal story is that children have that exclusive right even if such a right shall lead them, as in his case, nowhere and result in failure. So what matters is not the outcome but the principle of the individual's self-determination. This may sound absurd but nonetheless quite human. He advocates the freedom of children and uses his failure to prove its validity. This freedom gives power and pleasure to the individual but also leads him into his own and free annihilation, a paradox the reader can detect in the case of the second narrator and in that of Blear as well.

As said before, "From Far Away" is told by two narrators. The first narrator is remembering what happened at the table when the discussion and the narration by the second storyteller took place. As part of the discussion, therefore, comes the story told by the second narrator, who actually becomes the protagonist not only of his own story but of the first narrator's as well. And what is the first narrator's story? It is the entire narrative which includes the preliminary discussion of all those at the table plus the second narrator's tale. To intensify the technical confusion of narrative point of view, Benet allows the first narrator to tell not only what happened before and after the story of the second narrator, but actually to repeat verbatim the whole story of the latter. [14] So the second narrator is not actually the narrator now addressing the reader. The second narrator once addressed those at the table but later he is being repeated by the first and omniscient narrator, who is *now* recalling and relating the whole experience to the reader. Benet further enjoys his technical trick with the following inconsistency: on the one hand, the first narrator fails to remember the exact initial words which the second narrator used to start his story, and on the other, he is able to repeat with almost mechanical precision the rest of the story (94). Benet also makes his second narrator fail to determine accurately whether or not his confrontations with Blear were a clear reality or an experience afflicted and befogged by fantasy and dreams of fear and uncertainty (104). Again Benet has purposely undermined the reliability of the two characters as narrators, leaving the whole narration and its reality in conflict with its own mystery and enigma.

"An Incomplete Line"

César Abrantes, one of the main characters of this story, by the imposition of his sturdy and intransigent father, the famous industrialist of Región, Honorio Abrantes, finds himself in some sort of exile in England, where he studies mineralogy and has no foreseeable hope of returning to his hometown and family. Bored and tired of his present situation, one day César decides to marry a cultured young girl from his native Región, regardless of his father's strong opposition and readiness to disinherit him. Even though the father-son animosity was always poignant, the news of César's prospective marriage worsened it to the point of turning them into two permanent and deadly enemies whose chances for reconciliation were bleak, even when the wedding did not take place due to the bride's and her stepfather's mysterious disappearance. The narration takes an unexpected twist when César resorts to an English secret agency to look into his fiancée's sudden disappearance, which, because of the nature and special sequence of events, seems to have been caused either by death or elopement. From the information César gives, in English, to the two agents, whose literary counterparts are Sherlock Holmes and Dr. Watson,[15] a bizarre and complex labyrinth of emotions and family relations arise.

César and his fiancée both prove to be Honorio's illegitimate children, whom he procreated with women he deemed to be—as indeed they were—the economic assets for his industrial empire. At least from this bit of information the reader is able to infer some of the reasons for the father's adamant opposition to César's marriage—he was in fact marrying his own half-sister. It also appears that Honorio's ultimate purpose for keeping his son away from home and from his fiancée was pure greed, that is, to maintain absolute control and power over their (his children's) property or estates to which they would otherwise have been entitled to by law. Furthermore, it is also likely that he killed or somehow caused César's fiancée and her stepfather to disappear. Presumably the reason why his empire later collapsed and his life was plunged into despair was a result of his criminal and/or fraudulent behavior.[16]

A few elements of plot development remain unclear, and the narrator carefully obscures them with suggestions and contradictory suppositions that lead nowhere and totally invalidate the force of his narration. But whatever actually happened, the fact is that they are doomed, at the end, to endure an existence of oblivion, despair, and impotence as an end result of greedy and lusty behavior geared to the achievement of power.

The semiomniscient, third-person narrator, as in many of Benet's other narrations, is coldly detached from the story he presents and from its moral implications. It is as if his noncommittal attitude did not even allow him to search for more information and details which would have helped him and the reader to clarify the mystery of the characters' lives. The reader must cope not only with a slack narrator who does not search and gather enough information to tell the story, but also with a group of shadows trapped in their own moral and spiritual labyrinth. It is not necessary, however, to know exactly what happened. After all, the father's and son's deceitfulness forces their acts to remain in the darkness, and the narrator in turn has neither the desire nor the power to bring them into the open. In other words, their deceitfulness determines their lives and shapes the narrative wherein they evolve.

"Final Nights of a Damp Winter"

The death of his wife plunged Mr. Martín in a state of physical and mental confusion and distress, and since his bronchial illness worsened and symptoms of mental disorders began to emerge, his perceptive and diligent daughter suggested that he should take a vacation and rest. A resort somewhere in Levante was chosen as supposedly the ideal place for his health, and also for alleviating the loneliness of his widowerhood. Even though the weather was not so propitious for his health as expected, the daily presence of young female vacationers did help to subdue his loneliness and rejuvenate his heart—a bit too much, for he suddenly collapsed as a consequence of it. It all began when a young, attractive, sensual bather, running out of her bungalow, followed by a man, rushed into Mr. Martín's room and found a place to hide in his bathroom. She was wearing nothing, except a generous amount of suntan lotion and a towel tied around her breasts. Once the man was gone, Mr. Martín knocked on the door behind which she was hidden and announced that her pursuer "had just left" (165). To show him her gratitude, and as a reward for his help, she "rubbed his head— touching his neck lightly with the edge of her nail—and kissed him on the lips at the same time that, without failing to caress him, her hand slipped from his ear along his neck and collar bone" (166).

Benet's obvious technical trick played on the reader consists in breaking the pattern of his narration near the end of the story and thus immersing the reader in a reality different from the one he became accustomed to, from the beginning of the tale up until the change occurs (153–66). In the following section (166–69), events lose their normal sequence and consistency, and, by free association and subconscious bursts, the plot exposes, through Mr. Martín's "last dream," the multiple facets of his hidden and suppressed inner conflicts and emotions, mortally stirred by the caressing young girl. Here, the mother-wife-daughter-lover syndrome emerges, to over- whelm the dying character. The death of his wife, who was in his subconscious like a mother and a lover, left him alone, defenseless and insecure as a child. Who comes to fill the "vacuum" left by her? His daughter (156), and with the same "dedication" shown him when she was a child (156). That is, she does it with the same dedication she manifested when she needed his protection and love. Now that she is taking her mother's place, she feels the necessity to take care of him accordingly: she makes all the preliminary arrangements for his vacation, personally takes him to the resort, and even spends the first week with him until he gets settled in the new place.

In her absence, the "vacuum" recurs. He feels lonely and helpless again, although he tries hard to believe that he can take care of himself. Unexpectedly, this "vacuum" is filled by the young bather who tenderly caressed and kissed him, something she envisioned as a warm reward for his help. When the syndrome emerges in his mind while on the beach, the daughter reappears *through* the phone, distant, motionless, with no voice, and enclosed in a miniature frame, the same image she had of him (166). In his troubled mind, the bather and his daughter become interchangeable entities. One, in the absence of the other, fills the vacuum left by his wife. But he also must act as the father-lover figure who protects them against the harm of pursuers. Out of this interaction stems the tension that both endows the work with depth and eventually kills the protagonist. Needless to say, the absurd irony of the situation rests on the incongruity between his daughter's determination to protect and help him (she takes him to the beach) and the end result of that protection: his death.

The outer and inner realities of Mr. Martín, corresponding to the two sections of the story, have their own special stylistic and rhythmical patterns. The former is smooth and lineal, easy to follow and grasp its meaning, while the latter is chaotically more intense and fragmented, more difficult to apprehend. In the former, the language is more tenacious and captures a consistent and firm reality while in the latter the language becomes more hesitant and elliptical. Its meaning can be reached only "by dint of arduous conjectures" (168). Its hesitation is, in itself, the embodiment of the evanescent reality of Mr. Martín's dreams prior to his death. It is from this stylistic and psychological juxtaposition that stems the magic force of this story of lust and death, of innocent and incestuous love.

"Obiter Dictum"

"Obiter Dictum" forms part of a fictional police interrogation concerning the death of an insomniac, a drug-addict veteran with a persecution complex called Baretto. The one being interrogated is Mr. Gavilanes, also a veteran and Baretto's old acquaintance, who, while in town on a tour through the region, had accidentally run into his old fellow combatant and the next day had to report to the local police his tragic death. [17] "Obiter Dictum" is another of Benet's spectacular jokes wherein wit, irony, laughter, and sorrow are skillfully interwoven to entertain and disturb the reader in a nonchalant fashion.

The question of course is, who killed Baretto? Is this a homicide or a suicide? From the evidence gathered by the police, Baretto blew his own brains out with his own pistol, after he had written and delivered to the chief of police a note indicating that Gavilanes was in town and was after his life. As far as Gavilanes is concerned, he went to Baretto's apartment, found him on the floor of his bedroom, fired his gun, and missed him. But he missed the target and hit the floor because, at the moment he was pulling the trigger, he noticed that Baretto was already dead (183). It seems then that what the reader has before him is a truncated homicide and an induced, bizarre suicide. But the irony implicit in what has been said here is that this conclusion at which the police have arrived about the crime and its perpetrator actually precedes the interrogation, which is transcribed by Benet in "Obiter Dictum." From Gavilanes's confession—which for the reader is firsthand information since it comes directly from his mouth—one is led to believe that he is innocent. But from the information the police have already gathered, and which is not available directly to the reader, he is guilty of attempted murder and of inducing a person to commmit suicide. Furthermore, this is ironic because Gavilanes's poise and sometimes sarcastic attitude can be regarded as evidence both of his innocence and of a possible criminal experience that could have taught him that the best thing to do in like circumstances is to be relaxed and poised. So after the incident, not only did he call the police but he also cooperated and even helped them analyze all the possibilities surrounding the crime. He did not realize, however, that what he was doing was, in fact, helping to set his own trap. From what the police say, he was very sure that the crime was going to be carried out successfully. But in reality not only was he incapable of killing Baretto, but he ended up in the hands of the law. He intended to make Baretto his victim and ended up being, instead, the victim of his intended victim. Baretto is the winner because he planned his suicide very well.

"Obiter Dictum" can be viewed as two different and complementary texts. It is first, a fictional fragment of a regular police interrogation carefully transcribed—as if it were from a police file or tape. The dialogue—which forms the whole text of the "story" and appears in quotations—runs uninterrupted, without the intervention of a neutral narrator moderating the dialogue. As a fragment, the text is deliberately incomplete since it is a partial account of the crime and the ensuing incrimination of Gavilanes. It is *partial,* because we know only the police side and also the text itself opens up the possibility that there may be a mastermind working behind the scenes (182). Moreover, the first and last lines endorse the assertion that the text is an incomplete fragment. It begins with these words: "Let's proceed, starting from the point where we stopped yesterday" (173), and ends with the following: "Ah, if you so wish, Mr. Gavilanes . . ." (188). Notice how Benet intensifies the abruptness and mystery with which the dialogue is cut off by using the ellipses. Furthermore—as it was pointed out before—the incriminating evidence which the police have gathered against Gavilanes is not part of this text; the reader simply accepts as truth what the police say. The reader cannot form his own opinion since he had no firsthand information on which to base it. Also, Gavilanes's words are not necessarily self-incriminatory. What results from all this is that the entire interrogation is only a pretext for passing on to Gavilanes and to the reader what has already been decided. But this truncated text is also complete in the sense that it produces its full effect, that of showing through the police report how Gavilanes came to be held fully responsible for Baretto's death.

"Obiter Dictum" can also be viewed as a parody of a mystery story. In a mystery story, the author normally hands the reader the components (the pieces) of the mystery so that he may put them together and solve the mystery. In "Obiter Dictum," conversely, the components are already put together by the police and graciously handed to Gavilanes and to the reader. So what is the reader or Gavilanes supposed to do with the mystery already solved and his fate already decided? Nothing. Everything is already done. It is as if Benet would hand over not the pieces of the puzzle but the puzzle already assembled, and would later ask, is it not a good puzzle? Do you like it? The reader's traditional participation in solving the mystery is replaced in "Obiter Dictum" by the frustration or perplexity of the passive observer who has absolutely nothing to do or say. The situation is worse for Gavilanes because, likewise, he has nothing to do or say to save his skin, his fate has already been worked out—without his knowledge—by a diligent police or society.

"The Evil of Parity"

As in most of Benet's fiction, in "The Evil of Parity" action is minimal, and the reader accustomed to the narrative formulae of "and then what happened" will abandon the story on the first page. Benet's narratives withdraw from external action and reality in order to delve into the inner, troubled world of the characters (their hopes, the causes of their passivity and frustration) and later expose these to the reader in the same pristine elusiveness in which the afore-mentioned inner world was apprehended. It is this inner objective narrative method that makes Benet's art so complex and demanding.

In the story there are three characters: two men and a woman. It is hard at the beginning to tell who they are and what they are doing. Little by little, however, the reader learns some basic facts: that her name is Agueda and that she is about to die, that one of the two men almost certainly is her former rejected husband, and the other, Demetrio, perhaps her present lover. I say *perhaps* because there are also two complicating references on page 199 that vaguely suggest his being her second husband. Those references alude to her "second marital experience" and to her "first husband" as if Demetrio were now her second one. Agueda is a totally unfulfilled woman. Her sterility is her traumatic obsession that made her deceive and abandon her former husband for Demetrio, hoping to prove that the sterility was not her problem but his. When she finds that she cannot bear a child with Demetrio, she develops a guilt complex stemming from both her barren womanhood and her marital un-faithfulness and subsequent separation from her husband, to join his business partner, Demetrio. Ill and feeling death near, as if she were looking for reconciliation and forgiveness, she asks Demetrio to send her ex-husband the following telegram: "Agueda's health delicate. She begs you to come as soon as possible. Regards. Demetrio" (103). He decides to come. Demetrio picks him up at the train station, brings him home, and a close relation between the two is reborn while Agueda is paralyzed and forgotten in her room until her death. During all this time that the two men are together, it is as if she, forgotten in her loneliness, would already have been experiencing her death. The following proves this assertion. "Death surprised her while dreaming. . . . It did not even interrupt the pale conversation of two cups of coffee (of the two men chatting) . . . over her tomb was left an elongated pile of loose and dark dirt—of about the same proportions of her form in her bed" (205). When her ex-husband came, the two men began a new life. There-after their attitude toward her changed from a more positive one—before the men were reunited—to a more indifferent one. At the end, after she was buried, the two men came home—one holding the other's arm—sat at the table, and began to laugh, happy that she was finally gone (205–6).

Before his friend's arrival, Demetrio spent most of his time taking care of his ailing Agueda, putting aside all his business to assist her. But with the friend's arrival he mysteriously withdrew from her to devote time and attention to the newcomer. His indifference toward her becomes so intolerable for himself that he feels the necessity to take a ten-day business trip and leave Agueda in the "good hands" of her ex-husband (200). This trip is crucial in the structural development of the story, constituting the starting point of the unusual parity of their experiences in relation to Agueda and to each other. Just as Demetrio sent the telegram to his friend, picked him up at the train station, and brought him home, his friend—under similar circumstances—does the same for Demetrio. While Demetrio was away, his friend acted at home as if he were, again, Agueda's husband, as he used to be fifteen years ago; and Demetrio, returning home from the trip, felt the same way his friend felt when he was coming to see Agueda, desperate to be the one in control of the situation. Both, at home, feel an unusual secret jealousy over Agueda, a jealousy that draws them away from her to establish a mutual solidarity between the two; a solidarity of equal partnership, with a common future and a common woman, of whom they were the "co-owners" (204).

The complex network of emotions outlined here is a good example of what Benet can do with his narrative technique and poetic vision. He reaches the very soul of his characters. The mystery of their inner world emerges through a dynamic language that opens itself in multiple directions, in as many directions as there are emotions. The reading is as elusive as the reality in which the characters live and hide from each other. Benet does not leave reality as it normally is or appears to be; instead he systematically transforms it into a vague, formless shadow of itself wherein his spectral creatures dwell. Thus the transformation of the train, the station, and the passenger alighting (both at the beginning of the story and when Demetrio returns from his business trip) sets the tone of the dreamlike reality the reader and the characters themselves are to experience later on, especially the two men when they perceive the unreal and rare parity of their situations. For such transformation of reality, Benet resorts to a number of devices found in other works of his including the typical and disturbing long sentence, the confusion of identities, of who speaks or performs an action, the detemporalization and des-patialization of the action which seems to take place in a vacuum, the omission of details that might otherwise clarify the enigma, and the excessive inclusion of details that further intensify it. All of them make Benet's fiction unique, challenging, and aesthetically rewarding.

Chapter Seven
The Novel:
A Symphony of Despair

Benet has published thus far a total of five novels: *Volverás a Región* [You Will Return to Región, 1967], *Una meditación* [A Meditation, 1970], *Un viaje de invierno* [A Winter Journey, 1972], *La otra casa de Mazón* [The Mazóns' Other House, 1973], and *En el estado* [In the State, 1977]. With the exception of the last one, with which Benet moves away from Región to another similar area called La Portada, all take place in Región and vicinity. It is inaccurate and quite unnecessary to talk in terms of novelistic cycles or to try to classify rigorously Benet's literary output. For example, the unity of the trilogy seen by critics in the first three novels was suddenly expanded by the fourth. Should we now talk of a new unity or a tetralogy which in the future may become something else? Benet's world is so unique, so varied, and paradoxically so unified that it defies classification. Even in a novel such as *In The State,* which offers a departure from previous works in form, rhythm, and tone, his vision of man's perpetual ruin, solitude, and failure remains the same. Benet's fictional world as a whole is a symphony of despair, an organic composition with variants of form and execution.

You Will Return to Región: Playing with Ruins

You Will Return to Región is Benet's first major work of fiction. Like *You Will Never Get Anywhere,* the work passed basically unnoticed by critics and readers alike until 1969, when his second novel, *A Meditation,* was awarded the *Biblioteca Breve* Literary Prize. As Benet pointed out, the prize was a timely *consagración* ("recognition") that helped to attract people's attention not only to the prize-winning novel but to those other works he had previously written and published.[1] *You Will Return to Región* is an intricate body of fiction wherein most of the thematic and technical characteristics of *You Will Never Get Anywhere* reappear to be developed and manipulated with more intensity, skill, and vigor. It is in this novel, for instance, where Región, Benet's mythical, private novelistic cosmos (like Faulkner's Yoknapatawpha County or García Márquez's Macondo) is carefully and fully depicted and developed. With almost scientific and technical accuracy, the narrator presents its rivers, mountains, and complicated fauna and flora, while with intense metaphoric diction he portrays its ruin, fear, and solitude. Enigma again is the essence of the novel's artistic conception and development. Enigma is the cornerstone of the novel just as the novel is the cornerstone of Benet's fictional world. Its text was written five times between 1962 and 1965 and rejected an equal number of times by publishing houses which saw the lack of dialogue in the novel as a danger to any type of investment.[2]

You Will Return to Región[3] has, instead of a readily traceable plot in the traditional sense, two integrating and integrated situations which are briefly mentioned at the beginning of the novel, laconically developed throughout, and never clearly revealed in their entirety. The two situations are related first to the old Numa, who lives in the Sierra (mountains) and whose existence is felt by the people of Región only through the occasional echoes of his shooting (11), and second to the young gambler who, one night, "took away money and honor" from the town (11). Numa's "history" or "legend" is not clear. Some would say that he is an old Carlist war fighter, others that he is a monk and still others that he is simply a soldier, well known in Región who found refuge in the Sierra after losing his beloved (251). The enigma is further intensified by the fact that the people of the town themselves cannot determine if Numa's existence is part of objective reality, history, or simply a legend. What is certain is that he is there to kill anyone who dares enter the forest and that, by so doing, will keep the peace of mind of the town: "Do not ask me for anything else, I will kill him, that is it. This way your conscience will be always in peace and the forest under my sole control" (251). He is the guardian and "protector" of the state of ruin and solitude of the townsfolk. No intruder or disrupter of that state shall flee unchallenged. Critics have identified him with Franco.[4] Even though the interpretation may be plausible, it is too limiting and limited, since Numa, beyond historic reality, reaches universal significance: it is the evil force of destruction which impairs man's freedom. Numa is a symbol of death (11). No one knows or has seen him, but his reality is perceived through the deadly echo of his gun (12). On the other side, the gambler is the intruder who, by running away with Gamallo's money and woman, disturbed and brought about the decline of Región. A group of soldiers, horsemen and tracers, spurred on by vengeance, rushed after him into the Sierra: "Its decline is nothing but that, the memory and the cloud of dust from the cavalcade on the Torce road; the frenzy of an exhausted society, willing to believe it was going to retrieve its honor from a ravine of the Sierra; its pile of *nacre* pieces and its vengeance of blood" (11–12). Associated, one way or another, with the gambler are María Timoner, the woman with whom he ran away and by whom he presumably had a son; Gamallo, the "dishonored" soldier whose fiancée (María Timoner) eloped with the gambler and whose daughter later became, first, the mistress of María Timoner's son and then Doctor Sebastian's close friend. This labyrinthine configuration of human relations, running parallel with the labyrinthine topography and enigmatic aura of the Sierra where Numa is hidden (39), creates the overall impression of the entire novel as a human labyrinth. To understand the gambler's situation and its structural consequences one must detect the concept or idea which relates the incident to the decline of the town; this can be done, again, from a historical and a universal standpoint. It is basically "vengeance" that impels the horsemen against the gambler, the same force which moved Spain (Región) into the nightmare of the Civil War, one of the pillars of the novel (11).[5] After having defined the gambler's and Numa's situations as the two most important elements of novelistic plotting, it is now necessary to determine how they are developed and what their results are. The first references to the two situations are found at the very beginning of the novel and on the same page (11). The reader's attention and alertness have been stirred; he must now carefully follow the trend of thought laid down by the author when developing the two plot situations. The sporadic references to them paradoxically add something to their elucidation, but, by the same token, increase their aura of mystery. That is, the reader's interest increases as the enigma, set forth earlier, seems to be clearing up; yet, ironically, what was promising earlier proves at the end to be "disappointing," since those mysteries remain equally, if not more, puzzling. The question of Numa's identity is never answered, or, if it is, it is done through another mystery: he may be a Carlist fighter, a monk, or a Civil War soldier (251); this ambiguity helps to strengthen his mythical function in the novel. The recurrence of references to Numa and the gambler, in addition to creating a sense of structural unity in the novel, is a technical mechanism geared to alleviate intermittently the density of the work. It indirectly helps the reader in his journey through the book, appearing and disappearing like a light, as the cloudy inner thoughts of the characters flow. The most successful leitmotiv used in this respect is the shotgun's echo, associated with Numa's destructive and silence-restoring power. In the reader's mind, that echo is death; every time it reappears the connection is remembered. Quite masterfully it reaches its supreme poetic climax at the very end of the novel, to be specific, in its last two lines: "Through the two yelps of a lonely dog, a distant gunshot echo came to restore the eternal silence of the place" (315). This last recurrence fits perfectly at the end of the closing paragraph. The peace, or silence, of the house has been disrupted by the agitation produced by Sebastian's death, the departure of Gamallo's daughter, and the young man's struggled release. The echo of the shot arrives to restore the peace and silence of the house. The mere presence of these two situational recurrences (those of Numa and the gambler), one may say, makes the reader feel and visualize a novelistic pattern whereby the dynamics of the narrative follow the rise-fall rhythm of a wave. The reader must be alert to grasp the new bit of information each wave adds to complete the total current of the novel.

E. M. Forster, in his theory of plot, says that

> it requires mystery, but the mysteries are solved later on: the reader may be moving about in worlds unrealized, but the novelist has no misgivings. He is competent, poised above his work, throwing a beam of light here, popping on a cap of invisibility there, and (*qua* plot-maker) continually negotiating with himself *qua* character-monger as to the best effect to be produced. He plans his book beforehand: or anyhow he stands above it, his interest in cause and effect give him an air of predetermination.[6]

In the case of this novel, mystery, enigma, or labyrinth turn out to be not only the technical trait of its *plot* but, more important, an aspect of its *theme*. Life in Región, as it appears through the characters, is a complex idea and reality; it is an enigmatic experience which everyone is doomed to undergo. Furthermore, the solution of mystery predicted by Forster in a plot is, in Benet's *You Will Return to Región*, precisely the absence thereof. Its solution is its lack of solution. If the characters cannot find their way out of the labyrinth, if they cannot explain their existential fear, ruin, and solitude, neither can the novelist. And the reader must conform to it, since it is an aesthetically satisfying "solution." The opening two paragraphs of the novel back this interpretation. Anyone trying to reach the Sierra, sooner or later, will realize that each step toward his destination will inevitably move him away from it. And if there is someone who still persists, the only reality he will face is death. "He will, lying in the dust facing the sunset, watch how those beautiful, strange, black birds—which will destroy him—are circling up in the bare sky" (7). The more the characters struggle to understand and explain their past, present, and future, the more meaningless and nonsensical life seems to them. This is the tragic situation in which the two main characters, Gamallo's daugher and Doctor Sebastian, are trapped.

When referring to the labyrinthine nature of the Sierra as a reflection of the topography of Región and of the plot itself, the idea of a tense polarity is implied, explaining not only the antithetical inner nature of the characters—especially of the two most important ones—but also the total structure of the novel itself. The last three of the novel's four parts are devoted to the soliloquies of Sebastián and of Gamallo's daughter, who has come to his house before reaching Región. It seems as if she had stopped there on her way to that town (102–3). In one of her reflections, she says, "You do not find in me enough strength to continue on my journey and I do not find myself strong enough to abandon it. And all this is because we both look at the same situation from two somewhat different points of view. Both of them are grounded in fear; fear is something common to both of them, but I am sure that my fear is nothing but a bundle of conviction, while yours, which you are talking to me about, is nothing but the last stage before despair" (264). The same situation, the trip to Región, is looked upon by two people whose points of view are different: conviction and despair. She is still convinced that she can make it; Sebastian, on the verge of despair, knowing from experience the impossibility of the trip, thinks that she cannot. Fear is common to both: to her because her hopes may not come true and to him because her failure would cast him into total despair, since her failure would result in another proof of man's impotence.

The whole concept of journey or trip is here—and in many of Benet's other works—a metaphor of man's search for identity, of man's odyssey of exploration within his life and being, of his own labyrinth. The same idea of polarity appears in these characters' childhood: a schism of the individual between an instinctive desire and a traditional pattern of discipline. According to Sebastian, man goes through three developmental ages: (1) the instinctive age, (2) the age of reflection, which helps a person to justify what he had chosen in his early years, and (3) the age of despair and alienation, wherein man is urged to reject everything he has lived by since he finds it to be lacking motivation and justification. To live in peace one must refuse to enter the last age by struggling to remain in the second one: "My country, my people, my generation hardly glimpsed the first age, everything was given to us, we were scarcely able to choose anything" (254). The main repercussion of this concept of unfulfillment or existential incompleteness is, as he says, the cause of his present state of alienation. As was said, he finds himself on the brink of despair. The Jungian archetypal image of the destructive mother is present here; it is a threat to the developing individuality of Sebastian's childhood (130–32). The same overpowering image is also implicit in the case of Gamallo's daughter; her early years were lived under the iron control and protection of a covetous, inflexible, cruel governess, a figure later embodied in the victim's other protector: Adela, better know as Death (172–74). The archetype may also be regarded as an image of society, of civilization, of Spain.

Continuing with the discussion of polarity, it emerges that *You Will Return to Región* is a chronicle of the Spanish Civil War and a psychological treatment of the individual. Confrontation between the individual and society causes the human and stylistic tension of the work. The chronicler describes with precision and detail the stage and the war itself. Región and its Sierra—because of the way in which they are described—will remind the reader, with ironic overtones, of battlefields where heroically fought wars took place in antiquity. There is a "divortium aquarum" where Falangists and Republicans, riding old broken cars, previously used for delivering milk and firewood, were to fight. Because of the arrival of the winter, however, the confrontation did not occur, and—alluding to one of *Don Quijote*'s sarcastic passages—the two armies, "holding up their swords," had to await the spring (36). The individual side of the novel, in contrast to its social and external aspect, is con-

structed by Gamallo's daughter and Sebastián. Their present individual reality is the result of a series of anomalies experienced in
the past: one of these is the unfulfilled childhood deriving from the
supremacy of an inflexible traditional pattern of behavior and logic
over the individual's instinctive desires and appetites; another is the
loss of identity resulting from this antithetical situation plus the
Civil War. For those who—in one way or another—caused the war,
it became, says Sebastian, the opportunity to find peace in themselves, after a long history of turmoil and fermented bitterness. But
for those who found themselves thrown onto the battlefield, not
knowing why, the war was nothing but a traumatic experience
caused by confusion and fear (180). Finally, Gamallo's daughter says
that the lives of those who were brought up during the conflict
were doomed to lack a sense of future and purpose (159–60). Only
silence and death are left to them: "Ever since the war was over,"
she says, "I have imposed upon myself the discipline of silence"
(149). The two soliloquies, by their very nature, reflect such a
psychological and existential state of individual isolation. The psychological treatment of the individual, as opposed to the chronicle
of the Civil War, is developed by the characters themselves, by
their own introspection into their past, present, and future, into
their existence in relation to society and its realm of action, reaction,
and interaction. The author is absent. The most he does is moderate
their soliloquies. The reader is thus able to reach far into the actual
agitation of the characters' minds. Benet's technique of detachment
to present this aspect of the novel radically contrasts with the partly
traditional mode of depicting the war, where the narrator acts as
an "objective" chronicler. The manipulation of these two antithetical
styles becomes in itself an image of the problem in question: man's
inner and outer confrontation with society, with Spain in particular,
and civilization in general. It also materializes the permanent struggle between reason and instinct, a key theme of Benet's entire fiction.

     When the two main personages embark on an introspective jour-
ney to unfold their past, present, and future, what they think and
feel about these is clear: "Time," says Sebastian, "is the dimension
wherein a human being can only be unfortunate," and "since time
shows up only in man's misfortune, memory turns out to be only
the record of suffering. Time speaks only in terms of destiny, not
of what man will be but of something different from what he wishes
to be. That is why there is no future, and only an infinitesimal

fragment of the present is not the past" (257–58).[7] This nihilistic and gloomy conception of time bears two major consequences; here again the polarity of the work is revealed and thus reinforced. (1) Man's freedom, man's sense of self-definition, is overridden by external elements; that is, society has already determined the individual's future; man's present is the realization not of what was wanted by him, but of what was imposed by outer forces and, in this case, by the Civil War. In part, the state of silence in which the individual is to live or has chosen to live becomes a counteraction to his own destiny. The only redeeming concept of man's own emptiness is death. (2) If time is the dimension of man's misfortunes, that is, if time appears only in man's frustration, then man's perception of time is an assurance of his existential nothingness. For him, the only way to realize, understand, and measure time is through suffering. One may say that Sebastian's apothegm is: I suffer, therefore I am. Sebastian's language relating his pessimistic views on time reaches a high degree of suggestiveness through the repetitive use of the adverb "only" (five times in six lines); it expresses his conviction in what he says. His certainty is categorical.

One of the most striking stylistic devices Benet frequently employs here is, on the one hand, a seemingly linguistic verbosity evident in the almost never-ending sentence and the repetitive use of multiple subordinate clauses within the same sentence; and, on the other hand, a tendency toward an economy of information on what is occurring in the novel. The polar tension between a linguistic profusion and a conceptual economy reinforces the labyrinthine and enigmatic nature of the work and the character's life as well. The more he strives for an explanation of his existence, the more entangled he finds himself: anyone trying to reach the Sierra sooner or later will realize that each step toward his destination will inevitably move him away from it (7). The way Benet achieves this economy of information is so subtle and smooth that it may pass unnoticed. At times the narrator "gives" the bit of information, but accompanied by another alternative which negates any absolute certainty the former may introduce. For example, on page 19, a person has come to visit Adela and the boy with the thick glasses. At first that person appears to be a man; uncertainty is inserted when the narrator says, "or perhaps she came disguised under a man's coat and capped her head with a kerchief." The question is whether or not—in this very moment of great expectancy—that person is the boy's mother returning from the war. Later it is "suggested" that it was not his mother. As if the narrator himself did not know with absolute certainty, the word "perhaps" is frequently used to limit the information: Gamallo's daughter has come to see Sebastian, then "she took out of her purse a small leather billfold, and out of this, a card—an old yellowish, wrinkled card with its edges all worn out and dirty—(or was it perhaps a photograph?) which she handed to the doctor" (101). Two hundred pages later the truth about the item in question is revealed: it is a photograph (312). The fact that the "card" is mentioned first and in the normal flow of the sentence, and "photograph" later and only in parentheses, proves ironic and purposely misleading. Furthermore, the doubt implied here through the "perhaps" formula leads the reader to perceive the narrator's fallibility. His Olympian pose of omniscience has crumbled, as though the character's incapacity to reach any existential truth were also the narrator's.

To appreciate how functional the subordinate clause is in Benet's writings, an example is in order. The second paragraph of the novel—divided into three sentences—explains the lethal mystery of the Sierra, briefly stated in the introductory paragraph. The third sentence says, "Or else he will—tranquil, with no despair, permeated by a sort of indifference which does not leave him any room for reproach—let his last afternoon pass, [while] lying in the dust facing the sunset, watching those beautiful, strange, black birds, which will destroy him, circling up in the bare sky" (7). The poetic richness of this passage reveals Benet's skillful manipulation of language. The seeming verbosity of the sentence embodies an entire system of expression. The approaching end of the day and the approaching end of his life are poetically equivalent. Those "black" birds—which stand for death and night—will devour him. The circular structure of the sentence, echoing the image of the circling black birds, is achieved through the concepts of "indifference" and "lack of reproach" (on the part of the victim) which reach momentum in the last two lines where the narrator, as a casual by-the-way, inserts through the subordinate clause the individual's imminent death, "which will destroy him." The individual is watching how those birds are circling up in the sky. He does it without any outer sign of concern about his death. Death's inclusion in the sentence via a subordinate clause makes it look as if it were unimportant. Yet, quite ironically, it is the essence of the whole system of expression condensed in the sentence. Of course, from a strictly poetic point of view, the fact that he looks at the birds implies a look at death; but it is a look characterized by "indifference" and serenity. In the description of the mythical Sierra, to make the reader feel its destructive mystery which is a symbolic extension of the old Numa who lives there, the language is essentially vivid and dynamic. The great variety and personifying nature of the verbs and adjectives employed here force the reader to feel and literally see the presence of another mythical character, like the old Numa himself, molding man's destiny (40–49). And it is primarily this stylistic device which beautifully neutralizes the otherwise dragging and tedious pace of the topographic depiction of Región in the first part of the novel. But this slow pace in the description, instead of being a defect, as some critics have considered it to be,[8] is an essential ingredient quite pertinent to the conventional and descriptive function of the chronicler in the novel.

A Meditation: A Rambling Memory

Chronologically, *A Meditation* is Benet's second novel and aesthetically it is his best and most ambitious work.[9] Both in structure and style it is a complex, unique, and rich novel composed of only one paragraph, a 329-page paragraph, wherein the protagonist-narrator uninterruptedly and profusely pours out his recollections of, and reflections on, his past forty years. It is his hope that by embarking on this process of recollection and reflection of the past he will eventually understand better not only his own present and future, but also the present and future of his family, his friends, and his entire region, which is the symbol of both Spain and the world. The protagonist's undertaking is clearly as ambitious and colossal as Benet's own project of writing the novel itself.

His obsessed recollection has a traumatic event as its main frame of reference: the Spanish Civil War. This crisis endows his remembrances with a historical and objective consistency that ultimately secures the credibility and verisimilitude of the narrated material. Quite often the reader will find, in this respect, linguistic formulae such as "before," "during," or "after the war," used to locate in time a specific action. His memory strives to be as accurate as possible: when the war broke up—he says—"we were having a birthday party. I am mistaken, it was a christening party. My cousin

Cecilia had her second child" (39). He also remembers quite vividly
how relieved children felt when the crisis began because parents'
vigilance over them lessened as their concerns of war heightened.
He did not know then that this very tragedy would take away forever
an important group of people in his life (47). Even though the Civil
War is conspicuous in the work, the book does not emerge in any
way as a social or a political novel. In fact, its uniqueness again
defies classification.

In *A Meditation* no chronological sequence is followed and no
specific order, or priority of ideas, is observed. The massive networks
of actions and discussions emanate directly from the mobility and
intensity of his power of recollection and from his innate ability to
reflect and analyze every situation or problem independently from
or in relation to his present. As there are other characters in the
novel who have manias, such as Cayetano's for clocks and Jorge's
for burning rats and biting women's necks and lobes, the narrator's
involves reflecting on almost everything. As his recollection flows,
digressions, contradictions, hesitations, repetitions, and questionable value judgments are not only unavoidable but essential components of the narrative discourse of the monolithic text of the novel,
which has no chapters, no sections, and no paragraphs, except one:
that of the entire novel. In preparing the manuscript, the author
did not use the normal mechanism of separate pages, but one single
roll of paper, defying the patience of editors and readers alike. The
format of the pages produces a dismaying, vast, and visual monotony, a well-calculated effect, sought out by an unconventional author.

The direction of his discourse is not determined by a logical
sequence of exposition (cause-effect) but by the free flux of memory,
which turns the text into an uninterrupted, or continued, and fragmented monologue. It is uninterrupted because it moves along with
the accelerated flow of recollection, and it is fragmented due to the
multiple digressions, repetitions, and sudden change of memory's
direction. Between pages 29 and 35, for instance, the text is casually,
and one may say naturally, fragmented as follows: First, he remembers the time he hurt his knee on the way to the Ruan family home.
The incident automatically brings back the entire attraction and
admiration for his cousin Mary (29). Impelled by this special remembrance, he digresses on the nature and effects of memory and
time (29–33), which also is the theoretical exposition of the novelistic method implemented in *A Meditation.* Later, Mary is intro-

duced to the secrets of the rival Ruan family. Finally, the discourse is focused on how the members of that family used to play croquet (35). This textual disposition does not respond to a pattern of logical or normal exposition, but to an impulsive necessity of pure recollection. The narrator-protagonist cannot arrange his discourse according to the former, but can only transmit it to the reader as he receives it from, and is impelled by, the latter. To do otherwise would invalidate the effectiveness of his entire meditative process, whose continuity through fragmentation is the essence of his undertaking and of the structure of the novel. An identical fragmented continuity is found in Benet's typical sentence, which, more than in any other work, in *A Meditation* becomes structurally more meaningful since here it responds to, and captures thoroughly, the impulsive flow of memory. Both the entire text and the individual sentence in *A Meditation* are the image and the mirror of each other. The sentence is the structural and linguistic microcosm of the text and memory as a whole. The sentence is the novel in miniature. The sixteen lines of the middle sentence on page 239, for example, are fragmented in four different conceptual and affective units related in an elliptical fashion to his cousin Mary. Due to the very nature of recollection and meditation both the text in general and the sentence in particular must undergo a process of baroque transformation whereby they lose their normal linguistic and syntactical consistency in order to acquire the semantic intensity needed to support the exigencies of memory.

Talking about his narrator, his narrative discourse, and the novel itself, Benet says: *A Meditation* is an "excessively long and monotonous" work. "It is tedious. It had no dialogue and takes the form of a discourse, a long discourse. This discourse is a gentleman's memory. . . . This gentleman makes mistakes, confuses, and, above all, as a narrator of many things, he lies and shows in his own discourse his schemes, and therefore contradicts himself. . . . The discourse rests on an excessively cyclical pattern, because the character repeats himself in the anecdote he narrates. And after each narration, he digresses and engages in reflection about every situation, feeling and motivation; many of his reflections are prolix, boring, with great analytical pretensions which seem to make of the book an exceedingly farraginous volume."[10] Obviously, his remarks are purposely misleading for they are only partially true. Insofar as the text is concerned, indeed, it is a massive, long, and tedious discourse. Afer all, it embodies the unfolding of a nervous memory impelled to recapture a recent and distant past in all its details and complexities, and the reflections of a mature and psychologically obsessed mind also impelled to analyze each and every memory summoned by a demanding present. Thus what seems to be a textual deficiency is, in fact, a successful technical achievement. As one critic puts it: "Only by expanding language to its maximum potential can the narrator effectively say what he wants to say. His narrative style, therefore, must necessarily be lengthy, complex and circumlocutory."[11] Insofar as the narrator is concerned, Benet's assessment is likewise misleading. Obviously, he is playing and enjoying himself at the expense of his text and the reader by making statements that, in view of the formal configuration of the work, are not accurate.[12] Of course, his narrator repeats and contradicts himself often. True, he weaves together story and analysis and his prolixity becomes alienating and unbearable. But it is also true, however, that all these apparent deficiencies are, again, successful technical achievements for they respond to the very necessity of capturing the entire process of recollection. It is the only possible way the narrator can carry out his difficult task of rediscovering the past. He cannot stop and arrange his thoughts and emotions and then transmit them to the reader. He is only a passive intermediary between memory and reader. Memory controls him, not vice versa. And the inconsistencies of which he is guilty, and the mistakes he makes are the results of memory's fallibility.[13]

The first-person narrator employs a variety of methods to tell the story.[14] Often, he conveys the idea that what he is saying is true. For this, he uses formulae such as "I am sure" (174), "it is evident to me" (255), "I can still see it" (50), or "without a doubt" (322). At times he does not know or remember a fact or situation so he resorts to words like "I do not know" (28, 132), "I do not remember" (24, 50), or the ironic question, "How can I know it?" (199). When he doubts the veracity of his recollection he either says "maybe," "perhaps" (133, 308), or gives two alternatives, one of which, he is certain, has to be the truth (133) or at times, to convey the same uncertainty he simply says: "I imagine," "I suspect" (19, 315), or "if my memory is not mistaken" (55). Many times he is sure about the veracity of the facts but he decides to withhold the information because he wants to be discreet. So he uses words like "for reasons I am not going to tell" (234). If he has made a mistake, he recognizes his fallibility and proceeds to rectify it. When the Spanish Civil War broke out he says that his cousins and he were having a birthday party. But then he realizes that that is not true and says: "I am mistaken," it was a "christening party" (39). At times not only is he aware of the material he is narrating, but he is also in control of the process as well. So to this effect he uses statements like these: "As I already said" (316), "I repeat" (284), or "As it will be seen later (or it will not be seen, I think it does not make any difference)" (9). With the exception of this very last formula, the others reveal a conscious effort on the part of the narrator to be absolutely reliable, honest, discreet, and candid in his performance as a narrator. He tells what he knows, recognizes his fallibility, and rectifies mistakes. In synthesis, he wants to be believed.

In addition to these rhetorical devices of narrative point of view, two more merit special treatment: the direct transcription of manuscripts and of people's long and short statements, and the use of the first-person "I," as if he were an omniscient narrator. On his quest for full and accurate recovery of his past, the protagonist-narrator resorts on one occasion to a letter written by Cayetano Corral to his friend Carlos Bonaval (206–9). Besides adding an extra and reliable source of narrative information, the letter becomes a key parody of the novel in which it appears. This letter is a long, tedious, and dense discussion on the relations between physics and psychic phenomena. More than a friend's personal letter it is an impersonal philosophical treatise. To secure the authenticity of the manuscript and to suggest that he had direct access to it, the narrator specifies that the letter was about twenty pages long, that it was written on both sides of graph paper from a school notebook, and that the handwriting was small, sharp, and precise. Stylistically it resembles the text of the novel itself. The fragment, like the novel, is logically of one single paragraph. It is filled with scientific and pedantic terminology, parentheses, hyphens, long, exhausting sentences of up to nineteen lines, and foreign words. The haphazard ending of both, the fragment and the novel, is similar. Also the two *works* are *fragments* per se, the first of a letter, the second, of a recollection. The other transcriptions in the novel are of statements, brief or long, made by various characters. Like the letter, they help the narrator to enhance his veracity and reliability. But again, like the letter, they are subject to the same stylization, i.e., they conform to the same stylistic pattern the narrator employs for his entire

narrative, a literary maneuver that endangers the authenticity of the
transcripts because they seem to come out of the same mind and
pen as the rest of the novel. But the last and most serious blow to
the narrator's already questionable reliability is his sporadic performance as an omniscient narrator. That is, the "I" knows more
than he normally should, not only his own inner thoughts and
emotions, but those of others as well. This technical inconsistency
which sabotages narrative logic under the pretext of keeping up
with the exigencies of the free flow of memory is entirely appropriate
and effective in an ironic work such as *A Meditation*. In synthesis,
A Meditation becomes a self-destructive work, a work where its own
destruction is its own creation, and vice versa.[15] On the one hand,
Benet seeks to secure a reliable narrator, and on the other, he
undermines all the efforts.

As one may expect in a novel about the pursuit of the past such
as *A Meditation,* memory has to be the central force of the work.
And the question is, how does it operate or function in the novel?
To start with, reason sometimes conflicts with memory. When the
latter tells something, the former contradicts or simply does not
agree. The protagonist clearly *remembers* the last time he saw Mary's
fiancé. It was right before the war broke out. He (Mary's fiancé)
was wearing a white shirt, a short tie that did not even reach his
stomach, and was carrying a jacket under his arm. Moments before
leaving for Región, he squatted and began to talk and answer pa-
tiently all the children's questions (and the narrator was one of them);
then he walked away and disappeared on the other side of the
bannisters (90). The character realizes that, *logically,* that particular
occasion could not have been the last time he saw Mary's fiancé,
i.e., reason tells him that it was not. Memory, however, tells him
that it was: "and although there is no doubt that we saw him again,
that is the scene that—by all of reason's data and rebellion against—
passes to memory as the very last vision, after which the curtain of
exile draws on him" (50). The tension between a logical reason and
an emotional memory partially ends when he rejects the former and
goes along with the latter. And he is quite determined to go along
with it because memory actually replaces reason. To this effect he
says that that was the last time, because "I have not seen him again,"
even though reason had told him that he must have seen him again
(51). But what good does it do if he does not *remember* what reason
affirms, i.e., if the "other time" on which reason insists did not

have any impact on him and therefore was not recorded effectively in memory? By accepting the emotive truth of memory he must also undergo, as a consequence, another tension in his inner self. He feels both happy and unhappy about the content and meaning of that emotional truth. Happy, because now he relives, as a child, the very moments before the departure of Mary's fiancé. He relives the excitement he and the other children felt when he was answering all their questions. The excitement made him notice the distinctive color of his shirt, length of his tie, and place where he carried his jacket. And he feels unhappy, because now he realizes that that was the last time, that afterwards he would never see him again, that that was the beginning of the end of that person, the beginning of exile which, to the narrator, up to the time he relates, is like death itself.

Memory has its mysterious logic of association. The word *exile* is associated in his memory, and therefore in his life, with the scene or image (emotive image) of the last time he saw Mary's fiancé. *Exile* to him would be an abstract concept or an empty logical word (meaning the enforced or self-imposed and prolonged living away from one's country or community) without its emotional substance, i.e., without the composite image of the last time he saw him, which in turn is also meaningful to him because it affected a person, Mary, whom he always admired and to whom he felt an attraction ever since he hurt his knee when he was going with her to the Ruan family home (28–29). It may sound strange to the reader but natural and important to the character. In fact it is his "true obsession" (29).

To underline the conflict between the effects of memory and reason, the narrator states that "the same individual who scarcely remembers how he learned the multiplication table or heard for the first time a word of terror, will keep—until his death—the mark of his first terror or of the contact with the flesh of the opposite sex or the circumstances of an exam that measured his ability to study" (32). This leads him to another crucial remark which ultimately identifies and explains one of the very sources of both the nature of his recollection and the form of its expression. A remembrance, he thinks, is an emotional image in which other recurrent images are multiplied and begin to emerge from an entangled oblivion in order to produce a fragmented and free narration, jumping in time and space (32). The narrative is patterned by the free mobility of the images which multiply themselves and are recurrent. In view of this the *word* or *language* has to adjust itself to the *emotional image,* not vice versa. Consequently, *A Meditation* can never be "a narration where the action manifests itself to be logical and congruous" (33). In addition, in the novel, first comes the remembrance, the "resuscitation," or "resurrection," as Proust would say,[16] of moments past (events, situations, etc.), and all their wealth; then the reflections upon them. This does not mean the latter is not important; it is, in this case, because he is meditating on his past and not only recollecting it. The process of recollection is meaningful with his reflection. After all, he is striving to explain the present through an understanding of the past.

Memory's correlative concept is time and Benet deals with it in the novel by making his narrator reflect on it, and also by resorting to Cayetano's famous clock. Every time he looked at it, he would sense that its hands "would try to persuade him about his inevitable motionlessness despite his efforts to move in the chronological direction of time" (60). That is why we are today what we were yesterday and will be tomorrow what we are today: the same nothingness and emptiness (65). This conclusion has been reached by resurrecting the past and reflecting on it. This negative or gloomy outlook helps to build his own concept of memory as "the faculty of all suffering species that need to find out in part what they were in order to overcome the pain of what they are today" (52).[17] Memory becomes a means to know himself and a source of emotional relief since it helps him to alleviate and overcome the pain or suffering in the present. It is like a sedative to help with one's suffering of being an emptiness. Referring to his clock, Cayetano Corral is convinced that it does not measure time because time "was generated neither in the stars, nor in the clocks but in the tears" one sheds (71). One is aware of time only insofar as one suffers. Time is felt through one's own failure (71–72) and ruin. According to Cayetano, ". . . only disasters . . . are capable of marking time" (203). Time, says the narrator, echoing his friend Cayentano's perception, "is nothing but the capability of the body to bear misfortune" (81). Time, therefore, can be perceived even through mere fear of misfortune due to the relation established between the emotional image of fear of eventual misfortune and the very moment (time) in which such a fear is born in the individual's mind. So, for example, if a fear of war is born in me today, then I start to perceive time today because today is when I started to suffer at that fear. Time's correlative concept is love. Love possesses the possibility to overcome time, i.e., ruin, misery, and emptiness. But in *A Meditation,* the characters are incapable of loving. They are like animals limited only to the elemental orgiastic function of the genitals. This means they conquer time as long as orgasm lasts (294).[18] Once it is finished, they return to their previous state of temporality and dissatisfaction (294). There has been only a momentary fusion of bodies, not a lasting and spiritual union. Sex, more than a satisfaction, ends up being further evidence of their inherent failure. Their sexual act is a "thwarted attempt of fusion" (234). Unlike sexual instinct, love can detemporalize time, just as death can. But in *A Meditation,* love exists only in the reflections of the protagonist, not in the daily lives of other characters or presumably in his own (311–13).

A Meditation, perhaps more than Benet's other major novels, exhibits both a rich stylistic variety of text and a carefully executed unity of structure. From the interweaving of the two, stems the aesthetic excellence of the work as a whole. In addition to the stylistic and technical devices already studied and from which the aesthetic excellence derives, the following are of special interest.

Irony. Irony is one of the main unifying forces in the text. The narrator-protagonist decides to concentrate all his efforts upon recovering the past in order to analyze it and thus understand the present and the future. It is a journey in search of the self. Does he succeed? The answer is a metaphysical irony and enigma. He does, insofar as he discovers the truth (his truth) that the ruin and *la desesperanza* ("hopelessness" or "despair") of the present are the result of those of the past, and that those of the future shall be the rusult of those of the present (65). So the entire process of discovery, i.e, his whole 329-page paragraph, served to reveal to him the same *desesperanza* from where he started and of which he was already aware.[19] Did he really gain anything? No. It only added to his despair. His whole journey of discovery has resulted in an absurd Sisyphus-like activity, ending where he began and finding "consolation" in "hopelessness" (or "despair"), which is his ultimate reality (329). The entire irony of the protagonist's action is effectively stressed by ending the novel with the spectacular incongruity of the individual's finding "consolation" in "despair."

With a great deal of irony, Benet makes his character act as a reliable, quite dependable narrator and at the same time totally unreliable. Inevitably, this inconsistency undermines the veracity of the entire meditation, leaving the reader with a text which technically has no basis for commanding belief. Then, too, he is a person who does not like people when they disagree with him; if they do, it will affect his *trato* and *aprecio* ("treatment" and "esteem") toward them (226), and he himself recognizes it because he always wants to be *honest* in what he says. This is the same character who thinks that he has always been the victim, the scapegoat of everyone else (272), as if he were seeking, tacitly, compassion and understanding from the reader. Needless to say, all those inconsistencies and contradictions make him a simple and at the same time complex character and narrator.

As a result of the pervasive irony in the work, the reader must wonder if all those intricacies and psychophilosophical entanglements are nothing but the product of the narrator's banal verbosity or the ingredients of a spectacular joke played by the author at the expense of the reader and the character himself. The reader must also wonder why the narrator-protagonist, seemingly so perceptive of the meaning of people's actions, reactions, or interactions, so eloquent and alert, ends where he started. It appears too simplistic to say that he did what he did because that is the absurdity and the supreme irony of modern man. It is nonetheless true and perhaps the only answer.

The Grotesque.   The narrator elaborates situations that generate in the reader a clear "clash of incompatible reactions: laughter on the one hand and disgust on the other."[20] For instance, one night, Jorge goes to Camila's place to make love to her. He takes with him a dead rat in his coat pocket. Once ready in bed, he begins to excite her by biting the lobe of her ear, and as he ejaculates, blood starts to run down her cheek. Concomitantly, she feels his semen entering as he feels her blood flowing out. Before leaving the room he takes the rat from his pocket and carefuly places it on the pillow. Hours later, the Brabante lady takes the rat from the pillow and places it carefully on top of Camila's vagina. The reader's response is obviously two-fold: horror or disgust and laughter. And worse is the casual and sober manner in which the narrator describes it: "He bit the lobe of her ear—intensely, until he felt that his teeth made contact, separated only by a velum." Two incongruous actions are synchronized by revealing that the flowing of the semen coincided with the flowing of the blood. To the last minute of his visit the grotesque is present: "he left the room, after leaving on the pillow the cadaver of a rat that he had kept hidden until then in the pocket of his heavy woolen coat." Notice how the rat is humanized by calling its dead body a cadaver, and how the humanization of the rat coincides with the animalization of its owner. The grotesque scene reaches its peak, both conceptually and visually, when the Brabante lady "took the rat's cadaver and repeatedly caressed it . . . placed it, making a ball, over the covers right on top of the vagina." The grotesqueness of the scene is heightened by the ritual and dramatic form in which it is structured. It starts with the cannibalistic bite of the lobe, continues with the flowing of blood and semen, and ends with the union and identification of Camila's vagina with the rat, a union or symbolic transubstantiation performed by the priestess Brabante.

Needless to say, the grotesque elaboration of this episode has a definite purpose: to lower Jorge and Camila to the animal level and, conversely, elevate the rat to human status. In Jorge's deviant mind, Camila and the rat are the same. To play with or burn rats, as he normally does when he does not have Camila, produces the same sensation as having an orgasm with her (264, 269, 275). And the narrator is aware of the intrinsic nature of the situation. He points out that here, love and reason are closed, and instinct—like "the mouth," "the lips of the sex," "the hands," and "the bedroom"— is opened (143). He also explains clearly the symbolic relation of the rat with Camila's vagina (264), just in case the reader is not clever enough to discover it.[21] Furthermore, he reveals the origin of Jorge's obsession for rats and of his abnormal behavior with women. It all began when he saw a man whose hand was bitten by a rat which, in turn, was later bitten in its neck by the man trying to release his hand from the animal's teeth. The origin of his abnormal behavior is as grotesque as his subsequent manifestation with Camila, and the narrator not only describes the episode, but explains its psychological syndrome as if he were an expert on psychoanalysis or the interpretation of symbols. He does not leave it up to the reader but assumes it himself (266–67). In general, however, the grotesque episodes in the book offer no difficulty in the interpretation of their symbolic configuration. The *Indio,* for instance, who masturbates "three or four times in a row" during the winter and in front of his mother's picture, reveals a clear Oedipus complex, aroused by his insecurity recurrent every winter. Winter is the time he needs motherly protection. As in the scene with the rat, the *Indio*'s animalism is suggested when the beasts in the meadows are all frightened by his screams of pleasure emitted while ejaculating (155–56).

Besides these cases of clear grotesque stylization, there are others which, lacking the comic side, become gross actions that produce in the reader one unequivocal response, disgust or repulsion. Such is the *Indio*'s daily diet: "First, he put sugar in the palm of his hand which he emptied in his mouth, then he drank the potion in one gulp, and in the empty container he blew his nose using his fingers in order to fill it with his mucosities which he swallowed again" (260). Repulsion is the only possible reaction toward this individual's habit. Even though the *Indio*'s personality was already portrayed via his Oedipus complex, the narrator indulges himself remembering additional disorders in the same personage. Given the monotony of the novel, these grotesque stylizations do serve periodically to break that monotony and give the reader some sort of relief from the psychophilosophical intricacies and prolixities of the narrator.

Literary Creation and Criticism. As an important element of the book's ironic substructure, the narrator often judges actions and portrays individuals according to certain identifiable literary patterns with obvious parodic undertones. In other words, Benet, like, for instance, Goytisolo, Cabrera Infante or Carlos Fuentes, establishes a dialogue between his and other literary figures or texts, i.e., he makes literature with literature. Further, he makes of his text the theory and the practice of itself.

The reader has already been informed about Jorge's deviant behavior. Now what about him as a poet? As a result of his ironic and skeptical view of life, Jorge—says his friend the narrator—used to talk "with a great deal of sarcasm" about "the power of language" (268). He enjoyed "showing the grotesque aspects inherent in those who profess a pharisaic worship of the word" (268). And his own poetry was the target of his own critical furor. "I have never met"— says the narrator—"a writer who was so negative, so self-destructive and who was so festered by the image his work had created of him" (268). He had neither the desire nor the patience to talk about his own work. It bothered him tremendously when someone would bring it up, a trait reminiscent of Benet himself. As he used Camila or his rats to release his frustrations, resulting primarily from his own Oedipus complex, he employed his poetry as a weapon to revenge his father for some unknown offense inflicted on him. His art becomes the embodiment of his troubled inner self. In addition to Cayetano's letter to Carlos Bonaval, already studied earlier as a microcosmic reproduction of *A Meditation,* there are discussions which, within the novel, allude to its technical aspects. Remembering Carlos and Cayetano the narrator says, "I shall never fail to insist upon the type of conversation they were having at that particular moment. A long and interrupted, fragmented conversation that in order to look for its sentences it was necessary . . . to pick here and there the key word related to the former giving to it meaning thanks to an algebraical order different from and independent of the syntactical one" (157–58). Similarly, he continues comparing the algebraic order to the one used in "coded messages that some writers conceal in the labyrinth of their compositions" (157), coded messages that some writers—Benet in particular— conceal in the labyrinth of their works. Most of Benet's fiction, like the Cayetano-Carlos conversation, constitutes a long, fragmented monologue that, eschewing the normal syntactical order, adopts an algebraic system where one has to go back many lines, and even pages, in order to make the word connection and thus complete the sentence, the typical "unsyntactical marathon," "circumlocutory," "peripatetic," Benet-style sentence.[22] The narrator vowed "never to fail to insist" on the stylistic type of conversation between Cayetano and Carlos. He is obviously impressed by it, in fact, so impressed that he uses the same stylistic pattern of algebraic order to compose the text of his meditation. But as he is impressed by a particular style or mode of diction, he is equally critical of others. Discussing his female relatives' habits and peculiarities, he reveals that his aunt Isabel developed a nocturnal passion for the romantic Cuban poet Heredia. She used to sleep literally with his poetry, which became the cause not only of her barrenness but also of her demise. She died muttering French words she had borrowed from him (9, 17). Of course, the parody here has two victims, his aunt and her idol. In order to reinforce and expand the parodic effect, at first, people did not know if she was sleeping with Dumas's or Heredia's work. Later, the narrator found out that it was definitely with the latter's (9, 17). His displeasure and criticism also embrace the historical drama for being bombastic and pedestrian (203). He says, "Despite the fact that such historical dramas are staged in the towns of the peninsula when the heat grows stronger, they normally end cold and the curtain drops on an audience that, turning up lapels and collars and warming up their mouths with handkerchiefs," acts as if it were ready to accompany "the Princess's coffin on the way to her final rest" (203). And who are the actors in charge of performing this type of vulgar drama? "Some comedians of the [Spanish] language, most of whom were either stutterers or dwarfs" (203). With such actors, more than a serious historical drama, the play seems to be a puppet show or simply a farce.[23]

A *Winter Journey:* The Voice of a Nostalgic Consciousness

A *Winter Journey,* Benet's third novel,[24] is a complex and symbolic work that takes place somewhere near Región and sometime after the Spanish Civil War. Basically, it is about a lonely lady, Demetria, who seems to have been married to a man named Amat, and by whom she had a daughter, Coré. It is suggested that father and daughter have departed and that Demetria's only hope is to see at least her daughter back at the end of every March, when a party is to take place celebrating her return. As in most of the novels by Benet, in this one there are also multiple references to well-known families, personalities, and places from Región and the vicinity. The Mazón and Ruan families are briefly mentioned. Enrique Ruan from A *Meditation* reappears and so does the deadly Numa. References are also made to the Torce River, the Mantua forest, and the Pacientes road. This is to say, Benet resorts to some key names of people and places from his main fictional world of Región in order to make the reader feel, upon recognition, comfortable and secure in the strange world of the novel. Región's ruin, solitude, and death also reappear in this novel. But this does not mean that the novel as a whole is a mere repetition of Benet's previous fiction. Not at all. It is a new step in his art, another successful approach to his novelistic world of Región.

The image of a "winter journey" repeatedly has appeared throughout Benet's works of fiction and criticism. For instance, the narrator of A *Meditation* refers to a specific love story as "a winter journey to hell" (310). Later he uses the image of a "return from hell" and a "winter journey" to express man's futile existence (322, 327). The same image is used in *You Will Return to Región,* the journey of Gamallo's daughter to Sebastian's clinic to recover her individuality and thus overcome her solitude,[25] hopes which never materialized. But it was originally used in Benet's first book, *You Will Never Get Anywhere.* In the title novelette, Vicente's and Juan's journey through northern Europe, like the musician's in *A Winter Journey* to central Europe, represents man's odyssey into his turbulent inner self searching for his identity and the meaning of the world in which he is doomed to exist. The image seems to have always been in Benet's mind. It is found even in his critical writings. In the 1960s, he wrote an essay, "Op. Posth" (included now in *Door of Dust*), dealing with Schubert's personality and works. In it, Benet indicates that the German composer's *Die Winterreise* [A Winter Journey, 1827–28] is an artistic trap where Schubert had enshrouded under a traditional form "a great deal of that tone and sobriety which the members of the *schubertiaden* had always missed" (118–19). It is possible that while working on his essay on Franz Schubert, whom he greatly admires, Benet was also planning the construction of his *A Winter Journey,* where an anonymous wandering composer, perhaps Schubert himself, appears along with one of his waltzes, Waltz K, which not only becomes a recurrent image in the text but is reproduced at the end of the journey, forcing the reader to leave the world of the novel with the painful and monotonous sound of futility and despair emanating from the waltz that, in Benet's fictional piece, has been emptied of its original grace and splendor.

In an editorial note on Benet and his novel (preceding the actual text of the novel) is mentioned that its title, *A Winter Journey,* corresponds to the cycle Schubert composed in the last phase of his life, between 1827 and 1828, during the most devastating years of his life, ill, poor, and misunderstood, with nothing left but solitude and death. Schubert's *Die Winterreise* is a musicalization of twenty-four sentimental and second-rate poems written by his friend Wilhelm Muller (1794–1827). The points common to both Schubert's songs and the novel are (1) The tone and mood of solitude and despair. But in the former the solitude felt by the lover results from the absence of the beloved while in the latter it is felt by the mother because of her daughter's absence. (2) The ominous crow hovering in the songs as a symbol of death also persistently hovers in the novel. (3) The futility of the journey in the one is the structural core in the other. What matters here is not what they have in common, but the way Benet creates literature, conceiving and elaborating art with art, literature with music. So, more than a tribute to Schubert, *A Winter Journey* is a tribute to art per se.

The novel centers around the metaphor of the party or fiesta given annually by Demetria in celebration of her daughter's return at the end of March. In the opening paragraph, the omniscient narrator describes when and how the protagonist writes the invitations to her guests, and why she does it. It is learned that she writes them yearly during the first ten days of March, using the same formula, the same gray paper, and for the same guests. Her stern discipline and implacable sense of justice do not allow her to indulge herself in making changes (9–10). (The "gray" paper underlines the monotony of the whole affair). Mysteriously, in the next paragraph this same reality, clearly set up in the previous one, deteriorates and loses its consistency when the narrator states that at times Demetria has felt the urge to introduce some minor and last-minute changes so that the routine of the annual fiesta would not become a simple ritual, but rather a satisfying expression of her will (10–11). A polarity thus arises in her *fuero interno* (a concept that recurs throughout and becomes the equivalent to her consciousness). On the one hand, her "discipline and sense of justice force her not to deviate from the formula"; on the other, she wants the fiesta to be a direct manifestation of her will and "sovereignty" (10, 11, 15). How? By celebrating it according to her "entire satisfaction." This polarity becomes the key force affecting both the perception of reality and its formal portrayal.

Reality in *A Winter Journey* is, as indicated before, enigmatic and equivocal. It is in a constant state of suspense, evanescence, and flux, ready to be many things at once, all of which makes of the configuration of the text in itself an icon of the protagonist's hesitant, turbulent, and troubled mind. This is a novelistic world where nothing, absolutely nothing, is certain. It is as if everything would carry in its soul the seeds of its own elimination. Hope is futility, just as a possibility is an impossibility. In short, this is an ephemeral text, like a dream, portraying an evanescent reality that is at the same time, as the narrator states, history and legend (77). Amat appears to be her former husband yet he seems never to have existed. "Amat did not leave—but he was not there either—and he was not there before—because he had not left" (113). Coré, more than a product of Demetria's flesh, is of her fantasy (129). She probably does not live, yet the fiesta is being organized to honor her imagined return. From this angle, the fiesta seems to be an exteriorization of Demetria's frustrated motherhood. Every year she hopes her Coré will come, but she never does. This is a yearly renewed hope (Demetria's) that goes hand in hand with a yearly repeated futility.[26] Thus the fiesta, following this yearly cycle, has taken place, will take place, and, at the end of the novel, that is, at the end of this winter journey, is taking place either in reality or in the imagination. Clearly the reader perceives the opposition of forces that cancel each other out, leaving behind a long history of nothingness, of annual annulment; leaving behind a reality which is real to the degree that it is unreal. And the text in which it evolves is believable, not because, as the narrator puts it, that which is verisimilar is within that which is impossible (188) and that which is verisimilar has more meaning than that which is not (76). Demetria's hopes are real in the same degree that they are futile.

Subtlety is one of the methods of textual composition. It is through subtlety that the narrator builds the evanescent and mercurial reality. Says the narrator: "Outside herself 'possibly' there was not the smallest trace of Amat, nor was there of his former existence or of his present hypothetical whereabouts, nor of his passing by Región or by his house, nor much less of his legitimation as her husband" (191). "Possibly" is the key word that makes the reality outside Demetria's mind inapprehensible. It injects uncertainty. If it is "possible" that he does not exist *outside* Demetria's mind, it means that it is also "possible" that he does, and that possibly he does or does not exist *inside* her mind. So what is real? That which is exclusively *inside* or *outside* her mind? That he does and/or does not exist inside and/or outside her mind? Or simply the conflict taking place in her nostalgic and affective consciousness? And what is the "nostalgic consciousness" so often mentioned in the novel? To answer one must look into what is not the "nostalgic consciousness," that is, its antithesis: reason and some of its derivations: order, law, logic, and reflection. So the nostalgic consciousness has to do with the affective and instinctive side of man, which is in constant opposition to reason; opposition or tension that marks the rhythm and mood of the novel and, in general, of man's inner self. In one of the marginal notes[27] in the book it is said that "when the spirit renders meaning to things, it introduces a responsibility of meaning for itself. Reason renders meaning but the nostalgic consciousness sees only deceitfulness and treason in it." The nostalgic consciousness affirms that "he who renders meaning shall lose it for himself" (178). So reason not only deceives others but itself. It is a fraud and a mask, a facade (the often-mentioned *disfraz*) because that which logically seems to be an answer actually is not. As another marginal note synthesizes this idea, "everything is the opposite of what it appears to be" (45). The nostalgic consciousness is the animus, the impulse, the impetus, and courage to act without regard for reason and reflection (78). Demetria acts in her nostalgic consciousness moved by an instinctive force of mythical[28] recurrence, "The recurrence of an instinctive behavior banned by law," order, or logic (122). Logically, Coré will never come, nor will the nonexistent Amat. So logically her hope is futile.

A *Winter Journey,* as Ricardo Gullón explains, is the continuation and repetition of a myth, the myth of Demeter, whose daughter Kora (Persephone) was taken away by Pluto into the underworld and from where she would return, as in the novel, at the end of the winter and the beginning of the spring.[29] In the novel, as in the myth of Demeter, Demtria would isolate herself, to grieve and hope for her Persephone or Coré. Coré's return would end her winter existence. It seems that Demetria, in the novel, is an unmarried, frustrated woman who feels in her nostalgic consciousness (and the novel only exposes it, does not explain it) the mythical syndrome of sterility (winter)—fertility (spring) that is never solved or fulfilled, hence the despair, solitude, and death prevalent throughout the novel. It also seems that Amat, her actual or imagined husband, has abandoned her and has taken with him her actual or imagined daughter, turning Demetria into a vengeful and furious being, hence her nickname, *Nemesia* ("Nemesis")[30] by which she is known elsewhere. It is known that "she had sworn not to fail to pay that tribute to Amat" (63). Ever since he had left her and taken Coré away from Demetria's life, her land, and symbolically, herself, has become "barren and desolate" (63). Furthermore her sterility is like death itself, embodied in the cold, lifeless winter. People would call her, because of her dark clothes, *La oscura* ("The Dark One," 116). Her dark existence is reflected in her dark clothes and in the darkness of her house (131).

The novelistic space is not limited just to Demetria's nostalgic consciousness, but is also projected in her servant's, Arturo Bremont's, nostalgic consciousness. Again, he may be, like Coré, another product of Demetria's fantasy, yet he is the only other character with some degree of individual consistency and independence. Arturo acts, moved by both his own destiny and by Demetria's nostalgic consciousness, which is eager to substitute Coré and/or Amat with Arturo (and possibly vice versa). Following what Gullón's article says about the symbolic light suggested by his name, "Arturo," one may see that he has to leave when the party is about to begin because the spring light embodied in Coré is also about to arrive. But does this synchronic substitution of Arturo by Coré (and possibly, later on, of Coré by Arturo) occur at the end? No. Or possibly not. It seems that Coré does not arrive and that the fiesta is both the exequies for Demetria's dead hope and the celebration of the birth of another hope, or rather the rebirth of the same one, which again will result in nothing and thus continue the ritual repetition of life and death.

Arturo's perception of reality is as troubled and hesitant as Demetria's. Reality to him is as evanescent and ethereal as it is to her: "He had also seen her passing by on two or three occasions, or he had thought he had seen her or he had been told that that which he had and had not seen was her . . ." (63). Neither Demetria nor Arturo can arrive at any categorical conclusion about the perception, grasp, and apprehensibility of reality, but they do see, and so does the reader, that reality is one and many things at the same time. Benet's art does not allow a reality, or a situation, to be looked at from only one perspective, but from as many as is needed to portray it and transmit it in its wholeness, that is, in its nothingness.[31] Benet's language generates the illusion of existence through nonexistence. Arturo had seen her. But he is not sure whether it was on two or three occasions: He had been told that that which he had seen (reality) and not seen (unreality) was her (reality-unreality). Any external reality seen through the nostalgic consciousness of Demetria (or Arturo) must undergo the same process of derealization. For instance, La Gándara, Demetria's property, offers an oneiric perspective, an indefinably disgusting sensation. La Gándara is there, as if "hanging from the sky," as if having lost "forever the sense of verticality" (218–19). To get to her house, as one critic puts it, one "must decipher a complex maze of roads and pathways."[32] Space therefore has lost its consistency and stability, becoming a limbo of suspense and evanescence, a dream of indefinite mutability and uncertainty. As a result, it is impossible to determine *where*, and for that matter *when*, the action is taking place.

Time loses also its consistency[33] to the extent that past, present, and future are emptinesses that, insofar as man's destiny is concerned, do not differ from one another. One is as empty and meaningless as the others. But beneath this timeless time something crucial is taking place: "the infinitesimal decomposition of things, of whatever there was in Demetria's house." That "whatever" of course includes Demetria herself (82). So how can one tell that time passes? Through the infinitesimal decomposition of the self, through one's annihilation. No longer is time measured and marked by clocks, but by destruction. Clocks have been replaced by images of destruction, specifically by the "moth's inexorable, rigorous, chronometric and saturnine gnawing" (135). By contrast, a different symbol of permanence is employed: "The spirit of the porcelain" (30, 67, 232), something Demetria condemns and instinctively abhors, for she insists: "No, I do not want in my house porcelain nor metal objects, nothing that would last. Notice how here," she tells Arturo, "everything is unstable and putrescible, it is how it should be" (91). On another occasion she states that the one who would not be invited to her fiesta would be the spirit of the porcelain (231). As in Benet's other novels, time is marked by one's own annihilation. Just as the child of *A Tomb* would measure the passing of time through his own decomposition in the tomb in which he was destined to live, in *A Winter Journey* Demetria perceives its passing through her own "infinitesimal decomposition" in her dark and silent home, another symbolic extension of herself. Every day for Demetria is a monotonous "creature" like herself (44); an instant is as empty as a year, a decade, or a season (234); and past, present, and future are also concepts meaning nothing.

Benet builds his text not on a logical sequence of events but on a complex juxtaposition of narrative units usually developed around a specific recurrent image or symbol. Among the most important images are the fiesta and the journey of the guests to it; *El Bausán* (the straw doll); the horse; the musician and his papers, which seem to contain a composition of his (perhaps the Waltz K); the crows; the horseflies; the *Intruso* ("Intruder") and his woolen scarf; the Waltz K; the short circuits in Demetria's house; the transparent paper with the word AMAT on it; and, finally, the spirit of the porcelain already noted. With this symbolic variety the text acquires the metaphoric structure, complexity, and richness of a poem and the rhythmical pattern of a musical composition built on variety and repetition.

Fiesta, Guests, and Journey. Hostess and guests view the fiesta as a hope to redirect their empty existence. But their winter journey to the fiesta (in search of the spring) is both inevitable and futile. They are destined to come to the fiesta even if they already know that it will only plunge them into deeper frustration and anguish. They act like Sisyphus: to reach the top of the mountain (fiesta) is to see their hopes roll down and start all over again. The fiesta, besides confirming their futility, serves to mark time for them—a mythical rather than an arithmetical time, a nostalgic rather than a rational time (21). Since they attend impelled by a mythical instinct or collective-consciousness awareness one may suggest that the party as a symbol takes place in each individual's "nostalgic consciousness" and ultimately becomes the common destiny. The winter journey of the title is an ambiguous allusion to many things:[34] (1) Coré's departure and return; (2) Amat's departure and return; (3) the musician's trip to and return from central Europe; (4) Demetria's trip to and return from the printer of the invitations; (5) Arturo's trip to Demetria's house; (6) his departure heading to Mantúa; and (7) the arrival of a mysterious man called *El Intruso* and other guests who come to celebrate the arrival of Coré or Amat or both and/or Demetria's wedding. The journey image both endows the text with a minimum of mobility and expands the complex maze of narrative units, on whose juxtaposition and repetition rests ultimately the dreamlike configuration of the novel. Of the guests' journey one can neither follow accurately their sinuous and labyrinthine paths nor detect where or when they start or end, if they ever do. But the journey is the very essence of the novel's thematic and formal structure because each of the journeys mentioned above becomes the basis for each narrative unit.

"El Bausán." This small straw man symbolizes Demetria's sexual and maternal frustrations. The straw figure substitutes for Amat and Coré in her lonely and sterile existence (35, 205–6, 213).[35] Most of the time her *bausán* is on her lap, at times in between her legs (67), and once in a while against her breast, as if she were feeding it (128). In a novelistic context such as this one, where the four seasons are so important, the straw with which the doll or figure is stuffed is symbolic. It is Demetria's dead spring, a spring which is already fall. Only a dead spring is what Demetria has and must continue to have. The *bausán* is the substance of her own futility and permanent sterility, as is evident when the narrator states that a few pieces of straw remained in her breasts from when she had been kissing and holding the *bausán*. She had been holding and kissing it while watching her daughter being taken away on top of the sheaves of the funeral cart. The narrator suggests that Demetria's preparations for the fiesta, to receive her daughter, are like those of the mother who makes, ahead of time, all the clothes for the child who will never arrive (32–33).

The Horse.   The first and crucial time the horse is mentioned in the text is the following: "It is possible that at that time, in a meadow at the other side of the river, a horse, his front legs tied with a rope, was grazing. But this is only a possibility" (41). The narrator is not sure of it. The horse is, at this point, invisible, and furthermore his existence is uncertain. As the novel progresses, however, little by little, the horse becomes visible and is seen approaching the house, as if he were another guest invited to the fiesta (207). His origin is unknown, but here he is; a huge and healthy animal, full of life. Yet there is something mysterious about him: "one would say that he had an exuberance of energy, health and vitality, that his size was hiding the distressfulness of a corporeal frame that was as strong as it was useless, the melancholy of a desire that did not know how to find either expression or an outlet for its satisfaction" (216). On the one hand, the horse feels the joy of his strength; and on the other, the grief caused by an "indefinable weakness" (217). The horse, embodying the tragic tension of the individual, has its corporeal frame limited by the rope that impedes his action. The horse's appearance coincides with the end of winter and the beginning of spring. If his arrival is the arrival of spring, this is a spring which is already withered, for his instinctive fertility (spring) is impaired by the rope of futility. His arrival at the house, visualized by the penetration of his head through the window, is futile, just like the fiesta itself. Paradoxically, the horse's strength is also weakness. His body, because of the impairing rope, is a burden that he must drag, as though the unity of all the parts of his body had been broken. His vigor and strength are not enough either to drag those parts on or to pull them back together (219).

Musician, Horseflies, and Crows.   At this point three recurrent symbols must be studied with the horse image: the musician carrying the papers, "the blue [horse]flies," and the crows. On the same symbolic level, the horseflies and the crows follow the horse and man, respectively, becoming ominous symbols of death and futility accompanying the victims in their winter journey to the party. The victims are "at their mercy" (219). Like the flies of Machado's famous poem[36] "Las moscas," the horseflies and the crows in Benet's text are eternal, present from the beginning of man's journey to his death and even after, outliving him (190–91). Like the horse that has lost the unity of the parts of his body, the silent musician has lost the unity of his self, when we see him *a cuatro patas* ("on hands and knees"), sweating and crying, looking for the scattered pages (fragments) of his musical composition (240–41).[37] Accidentally (notice the influence of chance) he has dropped and lost control of his papers. Once fallen, some have become crumpled, others have been torn into pieces, and still others are lost. He is now unable to put the composition back together. Sweat and tears are the eloquent expressions of the impotence and frustration of horse and man. About the musician, the narrator says: "He was no longer capable of distinguishing the sweat from the tears or from the raindrops or from the dew, only one furious and blind bitterness had come to substitute every perception" (240). Benet's horse, like Picasso's horse in *Guernica,* would raise his head, snort with sudden rage, and taste his emptiness in his mouth. "Even though the night was cool, a drop of sweat appeared on his forelock, to later go down his face between his eye sockets finally to slip all the way to his lips" (219). At the very end of the novel the two victims symbolically merge, reaching the house where they refuse to look at each other. The musician, on his hands and knees, letting his tears flow ". . . did not look back to notice the presence of the horse . . ." (241).

The *Intruso* and the Woolen Scarf. Since the intruder knows that Demetria will never invite him to the party, he deliberately leaves his scarf in the room of the party so that he may have a reason to return next year. First, the scarf is a pretext the intruder employs to come to the party; as such, it is a *disfraz* ("facade") he uses to cover the inevitability of his journey to the party. Second, Demetria does not invite him because she realizes that the scarf, like the porcelain, "does not age" (63), it lasts; and nothing that lasts is welcomed in her house. But there is nothing she can do about it because they (scarf and porcelain) will always be there, just as the intruder will always return regardless of what his or her wishes are.

Third, the intruder and the scarf, on the one hand, and the guests and fiesta on the other, are subjects and objects of a ritual. They attend the party hoping for something but finding nothing, yet the process must repeat itself every year. The scarf and the party are eternally there for the intruder and the guests to come for them.[38]

The Waltz K. At the end of the book Benet reproduces the Waltz K. Above the facsimile there is an annotation in German which says: "Waltz composed by Franz Schubert on the occasion of his friend Leopold Kuppelwiesa's wedding to Johanna von Lutz on September 17th, 1826, preserved in the family Kuppelwiesa through tradition. Written down by Richard Strase. Quiet waltz-time."[39] Three interpretative points are suggested by the waltz: (1) Since it is played at the fiesta, which is among other things an evocative celebration of her real or imaginary wedding, the waltz is a means to imagine the reliving of a past she would like to exist, if it never existed; or, if it did exist, then the waltz is a means to reexperience that past. As said earlier, Amat may very well be, just like Coré, another product of her nostalgic consciousness. (2) It is a symbol of hope. With it, guests and hostess want to welcome and celebrate the arrival of spring, that is of Coré, of their own personal Coré. (3) The waltz is also the sound of death the individual hears in the journey and in the party, the musical background for the exequies at the death of his hopes (70), played not by a man but by the "catafalque" of the piano alone.

The other most important symbols are the *short circuit* that leaves Demetria's house in total darkness but which is fixed by Arturo, the restorer of life and order,[40] and the *transparent paper* on which the word AMAT had been written. Due to the transparency of the paper, AMAT is simultaneously TAMA. It is a "symbol of the dialectic between reason and instinct"[41] as well as a symbol of man's ritual of hope and futility. Again it is both life and death. AMAT means "loves," TAMA is the reverse reality of AMAT who "loves" and also MATA, "kills," a casual and serious play on the letters of the word (and life itself).

There are other special rhetorical devices employed in the elaboration of this enigmatic text. Irony, of foremost importance, results from the basic incongruity found in each character, between an affirmative intention and a negative outcome, between the possibility of realization and the inevitability of failure. The musician's journey to the musical capital of the world, Austria, in search of a possible realization of his dream results in failure and despair. The huge, vigorous body of the horse is only a nest of impotence. His strength is his weakness. The *bausán,* a means to alleviate Demetria's frustration, is also a means to perpetuate and intensify that frustration. The party, initially a symbol of hope, ends up being a symbol of death. The whole novelistic structure rests on irony. The absurd and the grotesque, extensions of the same fundamental irony mentioned above, are also decisive rhetorical devices geared to ridicule the same incongruity between hope and futility. To demonstrate this phenomenon, I have used three texts which complement each other and constitute one single narrative unit. Text I is the introduction and texts II and III, together, are the continuation and completion.

Text I. At the party, a sudden gust of wind struck a lady on the head. The narrator says that this blow "was not Numa's shot," but simply a breath of wind (death) that removed the hair from the lady's head (presumably Demetria), showing "a shiny and whitish skull." Amazed by her own "absurdity" she took a cup from a brass tray and, as she was lifting it to her mouth, her teeth fell out into the cup. They looked and sounded like the falling pearls from a necklace whose string had suddenly snapped. She could hardly verbalize through her bare gums that she had caught a cold. And the narrator continues: "Almost; and she did not sneeze. She made a face, her bald head and powdered face changed color and made a contraction like a piece of wet cloth ready to be squeezed, until two tears came out and a handkerchief appeared in front of her, producing a spasm that turned it [the handkerchief] into her own Verónica's Veil" (183–84). Through grotesque distortion, this handkerchief becomes the Verónica's Veil, and later the Brussels handkerchief that, dirty and wrinkled from constant use against her cold, Arturo must dispose of with the tips of two fingers (189). This grotesque and oneiric vision of the guests at the party is built on two significant and symbolic levels: (1) the actual decomposition of the self (falling teeth and hair); and (2) The Verónica's Veil, that is, the miraculous cloth that Verónica, a woman of Jerusalem, used, according to legend, to wipe the bleeding face of Christ on the way to his death on Calvary. These two symbols recur and complete themselves, forming two independent and yet complementary narrative units with texts II and III given below. Text II completes the image of decomposition and text III completes the Christ-Verónica image.

Text II says: "There was almost no light left. She could not distinguish them. From the floor she picked up a glass half filled with a very watery, yellowish liquid, at the bottom of which had been placed front and molar teeth, of the same color as that of the keyboard. An unbleached woolen scarf and, not too far away, almost invisible in the penumbra, a mass of tripes, intestinal worms, amoebas . . . fetuses, of the same cerulean color, that still alive, were entangling and contracting themselves in a painful, agonizing and nervous motion in order to adapt themselves to a geometric figure, under the sound of the fourth variation's last notes" (240). This narrative unit is the very center where many of the recurrent symbols already studied converge: here is the piano and its cerulean keyboard, of a color just like that of the teeth, the skull, the tripes, the worms, the amoebas, and the fetus (an expression of death). Here, like the parts of the horse's body and the scattered papers of the musician, the tripes and the other elements struggle vainly to regain some unity. The scarf, untouched, ageless, is witness to the decomposition of man, while the waltz serves as a musical background. In view of this, one may restate that the party is a ritual, a dance of death, and the house, the tomb where it is celebrated (remember its darkness and silence). The party, like death itself, is the only moment of truth when the *disfraces* ("masks" and "disguises") should fall and show what man really is in life and death: nothing (180). Taken as seen in both text I and text II, the decomposition image is completed. And the key rhetorical device unifying it is that of the grotesque in action. Indeed, from a technically grotesque depiction where repulsion and laughter go hand in hand (text I) the reader moves to a vision where, with the comic gone, repulsion and disgust are the main effects (text II). This second text contains an exclusively nauseous vision of death. It is as if, along with the individual, the rhetorical device of the grotesque would follow an inevitable progression of self-destruction. The reader begins with both laughter and repulsion, and ends only with the latter.

Text III is this: In a ". . . *regressus ad illo tempore,* the Babelic and telescopic Saint Anne, with the Virgin on her lap and the child in the arms of the latter," was accepting a cup of *espumoso* ("foamy drink") offered by a corporal of the Guardia Civil, as if sealing a pact between the Spanish Church and the State (180–81). Again, taking into account text I and text III, the image of Verónica is clearly effective due to the absurd and grotesque visualization of

Saint Anne holding the Virgin Mary and the Virgin Mary holding Christ; and the effect is heightened by the cup of *espumoso* that Saint Anne is graciously accepting from a *cabo* of the Guardia Civil. Text III is related to text I by the handkerchief Demetria used to wipe her nose, harassed by a severe cold, grotesquely transformed into her own Verónica cloth, equated with the cloth that Verónica used to wipe the bleeding face of Christ on his "journey" to death. So texts I and III allude to Saint Anne, the Virgin Mary, and Christ encountered by Verónica on his way to his death on Calvary. Reality by its own intensity turns into a grotesque vision of itself, the surreal image of what it actually is, once its mask has been removed by the indifferent, cold blow of death.

A *Winter Journey*, like most of Benet's other works, is built on a balance of intellectual and emotional complexity, the one formulated in the marginal annotations and the other interwoven with concepts in the main text. In the main text, concepts are uttered through the senses, especially sound, smell, sight, and touch. Three main objectives are accomplished: the proliferation of channels of perception of reality, here, of man's hopes and futility; the uncovering of the hidden vision of reality that lies beneath a mask; and, finally, the total exposition of the enigma of existence. To carry out this emotional exposition, for the reader's pleasure of the sense, Benet resorts to devices such as oxymoron, personification, synesthesia, etc.

Throughout the novel is found an ominous and persistent use of black. Demetria always wears a black shawl. Her house is in constant darkness. It seems that we see it only at night. When the reader moves away from the black, he finds himself with worn-out, faded colors. The whole novel seems to occur in an eternal penumbra. Colors, losing their consistency, are whitish, yellowish, or gray, never firm. In order to visualize her nothingness the narrator says that Demetria was seen by Arturo "stripped of time and colored by nothingness, simple juxtaposition of her figure with the colorless instant only represented by fear." And he continues that she was "insomniac and shadowless," so that on her "face there was not even a sign of a flesh touched by expectation" that she looked "atonic and almost white devoid of any emotion," and that with the "sudden arrival of cold, she would condense herself into . . . a black figure" (92–93). Note that she is colored by nothingness in a colorless instant, and casts no shadow; there is no color in her flesh, or if

there is any, it is off-white. This lifeless color of Demetria is condensed into her final black figure, which is death itself. Along with
the deterioration of the colors or the black or the caliginous penumbra, the air the characters breathe is vitiated. Arturo's room in
Demetria's house "exhaled the sticky and acid smell of his nightly
rest"; to make it worse, the room was dark and had almost no
ventilation. The ambience of the room, needless to say, is strange
and uncomfortable, which matches the rest of the house. To speak
of sound effects in the novel is to speak of silence so intense that
one can almost see it. And when something sounds, it is either
monotonous or distressing. The narrator says that the musician heard
in the Conservatory: "some practicing notes, three or four sole notes
with no continuation or rhythm, as if extracted from that emulative
effort of a vibrating chord" ready "to overcome the sadness of the
patio, to make perceptible to the eye—not to the ear—the vastness
of the loud laceration" (146).

Benet never fails to make good use of his narrative point of view,
a functional element that definitely intensifies the main problem
the characters encounter. Discussing this narrator requires delving
again into the technical core of the novel. The first problem the
reader encounters when opening the book on the first page of the
text is: whose are the comments in the margin? The narrator's or
the author's? In principle one must say they are the narrator's. But
why did he do it? Is he himself trying to decipher what he said in
the main text? Is he so impressed or so confused by what he said
that he has to make extra comments about it? It all seems that,
ironically, the narrator is trying to understand logically the text
that utters Demetria's nostalgic consciousness, as if he himself might
not have fully comprehended the labyrinth captured in the character
and transmitted to the reader in the main text. Obviously then,
those marginal notes do enhance the richness of the novel as a whole,
conveying either questions, categorical statements, principles,
syntheses, conclusions, or mere observations that, at times, confuse
more than help.

This third-person narrator acts with a considerable degree of inconsistency which of course is typical of Benet's narrators. In *A
Winter Journey,* the narrator not only relates what a character does,
thinks, hopes, or feels, but also comments, makes value judgments,
and, in order to explain a given situation, resorts to similes that
normally entangle the matter more than clarify it. One of the main

similes in the novel is the mother and her first-born. He relates the narrative material, as indicated before, not in a logical or chronological fashion and spatial order but according to the dynamics of the character's nostalgic consciousness or affective or instinctive logic. His omniscience is limited, and he must operate within that framework. Furthermore, his narrative task is an exploration of an area he knows no more or less than the character himself, so that he acts in a limited way. Benet sacrifices consistency in narrative point of view in order to achieve special effects that justify fully that inconsistency. And paradoxically, it enhances the veracity of the narration.

This and other effects are evident in these instances. When the narrator is not sure about something, he strives to appear honest by using formulae that reveal such an uncertainty. Referring to the horse, he says: "It is possible that, at that time, in a meadow at the other side of the river, a horse, his front legs tied with a rope, was grazing. But this is only a possibility" (41). He underlines his uncertainty by repeating the idea of "possibility." If he knows other things which are more unlikely for him to know, why does he not know this? Why does he act as an unomniscient narrator? The answer is found in the second reference to the horse (58–59). Here the horse is visible for the first time. Before, his presence in the meadow was only a possibility; now the horse is a reality, but an "unreal" reality, the narrator specifies, because it is seen with no shadow, no weight, no verticality. And it could not walk or jump, but only slide. So what Benet has done is break the consistency of narrative point of view, make his narrator appear very limited in his omniscience, generating thereby the unreal reality and mysterious aura of the horse. If he had known everything about the horse in the first reference, then the whole enigma of it would have vanished.

A similar effect stems from the narrator's lack of information on the *Intruso,* concerning whom the most he can do is relate what people say or think about him, to repeat the hypotheses people have created about him (109–11). The *Intruso* is a *leyenda local,* a "local legend," whose origin neither the author nor the narrator nor even the townspeople are in the position to know. So the *Intruso* must remain as a pure legend, but a legend more real than any other individual who has a clear history of his existence. As a result the narrative process becomes a learning process for the narrator and for the reader.

There are times when the third-person narrator suddenly, without warning, switches to a blurred first-person narrator who appears to be almost an impersonal subject. In such cases the narration is left with no identifiable narrative voice. For instance, who is the narrative person who in the middle of page 172 says: "Yes, as always, it is the nostalgic consciousness's fault—that immature and never satisfied creature—that does not know how to follow the steps of reason without repeating, day afer day, the same old questions. . . ." Is it Arturo? the narrator? or Demetria? Still worse, on the next page (173), the first question about the party is left in the air, without a questioning subject. From the *tú* form (informal you) it appears that the question is Demetria's, but unlike the last time she spoke, on the preceding page (172), here she is not quoted. In view of this, one may view the text itself as an evanescent body of symbols, coded units, without subjects to whom to attribute them, wandering in a limbo like the reality they express. The narrator uses several formulae to signal the reader that he is in full control of his narration, for instance, "It should be remembered that . . ." (83), or "it should be understood that," etc. (27). Yet in one of his marginal annotations about the horse, (assuming those annotations are his), he states that "In this respect nothing is known for sure" (41), suggesting that indeed what the text says is absolutely true, thus heightening its reliability through its veracity: he knows that nothing else is known about the specific subject with which he deals in the main text.

The Mazóns' Other House: Drama and Tragedy of Ruin

Benet's fourth major novel, *The Mazóns' Other House,* is both a departure from and a continuation or expansion of the Región world of fiction. It is a departure because of its text's dual composition, combining narrative and drama or tragedy and comedy, as Benet suggests.[42] And it is a continuation in view of the recurrence of typical themes, characters, and places. The protagonist in *A Meditation* regretfully says, "How little we knew at that time, for our inner limited selves, that our family also had the sign that, like the suicidal compulsion of the Mazón family or the Llanes' frivolity or the Gros' pride and fatalism, was going to brand and accompany us in our destiny which was led precisely by a knowledge that, without being part of it, determines the force unknown to us." *The*

Mazóns' Other House is the novelistic close-up of the family's downfall or suicide. The title alludes to the family's original house in the town of El Auge. The second house in Región was founded by Eugenio after he ran away from his family. The portrait of the family's ruin is an experiment in expanding and sharpening the author's view and the reader's perception of man's solitude and deterioration in the mythical town of Región and its surroundings. The same deception, animosity, and distrust so deeply felt and experienced by families and other social groups in the area are those factors which drive the Mazón family to alienation and destruction. They senselessly blame each other. Clara accuses Cristino for having "crucified" his family; Cristino, in turn, cannot understand how he could be responsible, since he was merely a member of this "sick family" (94, 97). They waste time and energy trying to find the culprit rather than rebuild the family. The reader, on the other hand, finds himself in a situation whereby the total experience of the family breakdown undermines the need for holding anyone responsible for it.

The novel commences with a fragment of the Book of Jonah (chap. 4) whose purpose is to anticipate the philosophical problem of the work: the tension between the forces of life and death, between God's protection and abandonment of man. This is, at least, what the five transcribed verses in the novel suggest. From the remaining six, however, which were not included but which complete the sense of the chapter and the biblical passage as well, that tension is provoked by man's annoyance and indignation with God for his divine inconsistency when he did not destroy Nineveh as he had promised. In both cases, man's impotence and absurdity emerged as his two most distinctive characteristics: his impotence derives from the fact that he cannot stop God's arbitrary help and abandonment; his absurdity, from his complaining to God for not destroying man as promised. These introductory biblical verses are followed by two major parts: the narrative and the dramatic units. The narrative unit is fragmented into five pieces, each becoming the preface of each scene in the drama.

This ambivalent structure opens three different, yet complementary, approaches for the reader's perception of the work: (1) he may proceed with the preface, omitting the drama; (2) he may limit himself to the drama, leaving out the narrative; and (3) he may go from one form to another, as the book is, in fact, set up. These three alternatives become viable channels of perception because the narrative, the drama, and the narrative with the drama, each using, respectively, past, present, and past and present combined (as a unified concept of time), of the family, lead the reader to the same: the discovery of the Mazóns' downfall. It is safe to say that *The Mazóns' Other House* is a triptych of mirrors where destruction is its common image. The characters are convinced that the only sign of continuity in time is destruction. "I can understand neither the order of things nor their laws, and it is only fair to think that we die every night, that there is no other possible continuity" (219), is what Yosen admits after assessing the meaning of his existence. Explaining the physical condition of the family house, the narrator says, quite pertinently to what is being studied here, that only the weather has graciously accepted the gift of debris, not to pursue its demolition but to preserve—thanks to its dryness—the painful and unstable equilibrium which was gained in the past by fire and arms (12).

The symbolism of the house is clear: its state of destruction is static; it is the same today as it was yesterday and will be tomorrow. Its shaky equilibrium is the one and only principle governing its condition. Since time, paradoxically, preserves destruction from destruction, the history of the house, and of Spain, is a boring, never-ending repetition of the same thing; therefore, as Cristino puts it, it lacks interest (104). As in *You Will Return to Región,* in *The Mazóns' Other House* time is the recorder of man's suffering, and the distinction between past and present for man's perception of his ruin is inconsequential. To mitigate his pain and avoid despair, the individual must play the game of life, must subdue his acts to the vagaries of chance: "Roll the dice, Eugenia, I am trying to console myself," Cristino requests of his partner (47).

The Narrative Unit. The omniscient narrator of this unit pretends to be an objective historian who seeks to create a detailed and reliable picture of the family's past, based upon facts with precise location in time and space. Descriptive references to places and implied accuracy in the information about the year in which an event occurs are abundant (66–67). One feels how the narrator builds, step by step, in architechtonic fashion, the past, the destruction of the Mazóns. Beginning with the geographic location of the house, and proceeding to the arrival and extinction of the first and second generations, the account concludes with the disbandment of the third. Cristino, seen in the fall of 1954 throughout the drama, seems to be the only survivor; but rather than a sign of hope, he is the evidence of the family's sickness. As in his other works of fiction, Benet's artistic sabotage, here, is part of his novelistic creation. The historical veracity and its architectonic expression in the narrative unit of *The Mazóns' Other House* is an element of the chaotic and labyrinthine configuration which embodies the theme of destruction and suggests the author's constant endeavor to create enigmatic literature. The tension between the formal creation and destruction of this section is the artistic extension of the family's history as well as of man's destiny, as was anticipated by the prefatory biblical verses, where Jonah was victimized by a protective and destructive God.

Benet manipulates a variety of stylistic devices to diffuse historical veracity. The family tree, instead of aiding the reader and the characters themselves to know who is who and who his progenitors are, is an oneiric jumble of family relations where many members are not aware of their own identity, since their origin may be a clandestine relation or incest (66–67, 73). Even though names are used to identify the characters, there are cases, such as those of Clara and Eugenio, where, given the family's tradition of naming several persons with the same name, it is almost impossible to distinguish among them. Furthermore, it is questionable whether or not the reader is even dealing with the Mazón family, since at one point some of its predecessors, the old muleteer and the woman whom he saved from drowning, deliberately never confided their real names to anyone (66). To enhance the mysterious and alienating nature of the characters' world, Benet consistently eliminates the intelligibility of the sentence by fragmenting and crowding it with many and lengthy subordinate clauses which, ironically, instead of clarifying as their traditional function demands, only confuse the statement.

The one single sentence which is the entire second paragraph— one and a half pages—of the novel has seven relative clauses. Although each adds new information which leads to the better understanding of the main sentence, they distract the reader's attention from its content. If one is to delve further into this phenomenon, he will appreciate Benet's artistic skills. The principal sentence put together is this: "Of all those patterns of life they try to establish and develop in the country only those which impose a rudimentary and regressive way of survival prevailed" (11–12). The first half of the sentence stops with the word "country" and the reader's curiosity at this point is spurred by wondering what patterns of life actually flourished in the country. Only after a very long pause and suspense is that curiosity satisfied. The sentence, more than a statement, functions as a question-answer mechanism. In the same narrative unit of the novel, as is true in most of Benet's works, the frequent use of pronouns or indefinite articles and the deliberate omission of subjects or particles which in one way or another may reveal who the performer of the action is constitute other auxiliary forms of dimming and finally extinguishing the identity of the character, thereby reinforcing the ambiguity of his world. What the reader realizes and senses is that here man's identity, just like the Mazón family and its house, is only an embodiment of destruction. The phantom members of the family are like their dilapidated and haunted house; its description is symbolically appropriate: "outside walls with no interior, tumbled-down windows facing a heap of roof tiles and whitewashed beams" (12).

The Dramatic Unit.   The five scenes of this drama begin with an informative note concerning the location of the action in time (fall of 1954) and space (the house) and the "blurred and unintelligible" nature of the characters (29). But, besides being a simple informative note contained in one single sentence, it also turns out to be an incomplete *dramatis personae,* listing some of the characters and omitting the names of four: Clara, José, Eugenio, and Carlos Mazón. Considering this unit from the point of view of dramatic action, almost nothing happens in the five scenes. Cristino Mazón is talking to, or rather at, Eugenia Fernández in the kitchen; they seem to be fearfully waiting for something to occur or for someone to come. With the cold wintry night approaching, their fear increases. In the middle of their conversation, a grotesque medieval-modern king enters. The expectation heightens. The other members of the family arrive, accusing Cristino of its downfall. José and Carlos Mazón finally leave, and the echo of a gun (Numa's) is heard from the Sierra. In addition to the special nature of this motionless action, reduced to nonsensical conversation, the author strips the play, if one is to see this amorphous composition as a play, of all dramatic or theatrical ingredients which could interfere with the characters' obsessive discussion of their fear and frustration in the intimacy of the kitchen were they remain seated. Since they do nothing except play dice, the stage directions are confined almost entirely to the beginning of the scenes for purposes of stating that the action remains in the same place or that new characters have arrived.

Contrary to the narrative part of the novel, here the reader perceives directly from the characters their perpetual state of ruin, not only from what they say about themselves, their family strifes, their society and values, but also from the contradictory and absurd way they converse, which, more than a logical act of communication, becomes an ominous dialogue of the dead, a dialogue nonetheless meaningful to the reality of which they are a part. It is their conviction that life is a futile game where chance, not reason, directs the course of events. It is hard to accept, says the king, "that the human race still continues to believe in an order governed by reason. . . . Wouldn't it be wiser to rely on chance, whereby any absurdity would make some sense?" (155).

Without losing its universal scope, the main target of Benet's critical view is also Spain, with its ethical, social, and political values. The king, who thinks of himself as a feudal symbol of tradition, owes his respect not to his father but to his master, the old Numa, Franco (100). Even though he enters as a medieval king, he is portrayed as Juan Carlos in his submissive role as head of state. Yosen, alluding to Franco's power, predicts the confusion that will follow the death of the person who "for years has been the one infallible leader" (143). Submission and conformity are the pattern of behavior, from the king down to the masses. "I have never done anything," says Cristino, realizing his impotence. "I have not moved a finger to change things. Wouldn't he [Numa] [Franco] be pleased with me?" (167). Everyone knows what he himself is and what his role is: nothing and none, respectively. What is ironic and absurd is that class consciousness and *machismo* still emerge as national idiosyncracies. Eugenia Fernández, the aging servant, must accept her master Cristino's truth: "three is five" (48). Believing that there are differences between himself and Eugenia, he says, "I am high class. High in everything" (36). "My race has a mission, Eugenia, to govern and subdue the rest" (41). Furthermore, "the fact that we share the same lot of suffering is an inconvenience that . . . fills me with loathing and drags me to despair" (49). What this does to the character is to alienate him further, since any potential communication is shattered. A double question arises here. Is this confinement of the character to his snail's shell of pride a positive and praiseworthy sign of his individual strength, disregarding, of course, the immorality of his pretension? Or is it simply another of Benet's moves to expose the stupidity of the character, adding another dimension and intensifying the absurdity of life, thereby to suggest to the reader the nature of the work he is dealing with? Everything seems to point to the second possibility. It must be emphasized that Cristino's inconsistency (and also the king's) between the prejudiced, medieval mind and the modern existential view produces the same overall effect of absurdity: absurdity as another manifestation of ruin and destruction, the unifying concept of *The Mazóns' Other House.*

The Narrative and Dramatic Fusion.   Because both narrative and dramatic units are fragmented in a number of alternating subunits, the reader's active participation in the creative process is required. His attention must be concurrently focused upon two different, yet identical, worlds, confronting two different manners of expression for the same material. Furthermore, by setting up the fragments in an alternating fashion, the Mazón family's perpetual suicide is visible intermittently through its past and present, through the victim's actions and thoughts. The one and only reality met anywhere, any time, and in any way, like a malignant ubiquity, is destruction and ruin, with all of their consequences bearing upon the individual's conception of himself, time, and the world. The transition from narrative to dramatic form generates a unique treatment of narrative point of view in the work. The source of information being, on the one hand, a limited third-person narrator and, on the other, the characters themselves, the reader has no choice but to accept the inevitable *truth* about the family's *ruin.* The potential unreliability of the former is mitigated by the characters' direct information about themselves to the reader, since that information coincides with the truth revealed by the semiomniscient narrator. Thus, narrator and character mutually reinforce their veracity and reliability. Both using their own distinctive means have discovered for the reader the same, exact reality of ruin and solitude. But while the narrator is cognizant of the discovery process and of the actual communication of its outcome to the reader, the character is not. He is aware of his ruin, of course, but not of its being explored and exposed by the narrator and by himself as a character for the reader.

In the State: In Search of a New Beginning

In the State, more than a mature achievement, the work seems to be an amorphous experimental step taken by an author desperate to find a new novel, different from those he has been producing for more than a decade.[43] *In the State* is a fragmented narrative discourse of eighteen irregularly developed chapters where language becomes an end in itself, where plot and portrayal of characters do not count, and the consistency of time and space is eliminated. Región has been here replaced by another mythical place, La Portada, an isolated, miserable flatland whose visual monotony is barely altered by the presence of a lonely elm and a few inns sheltering a handful of surviving specters. Besides deterioration and ruin, also prevalent in Región, in La Portada solitude is the other adversity overwhelming man and nature. This inhospitable, arid land, immoderately cold and hot, is regarded by the narrator with malice as the ideal place for "contemplation, meditation and brutalization" (211), an Arcadia reserved for idiots or "heroes" (209) willing to devote themselves to "spiritual functions" (210). Like Región, La Portada, "the most inhospitable corner in the most unfortunate and abominable land in the West" (160), is obviously a parodic symbol of Spain, more specifically of the Castilian region, the heart of the nation. Most of its description is reminiscent of the emotive details used by some members of the Generation of 1898 (especially Azorín) who sought in his works the so-called essence and spirit of the Castilian landscape and thus of Spain itself.

To this land of meditation and brutalization come the three main characters in the novel, Mr. Hervás, Mrs. Somer, and her son-in-law, Ricardo. Their absurd intention is to spend in La Portada a couple of weeks of vaction and relaxation, away from the turbulent and stifling routine of the city. The novel opens with a clear description of their arrival in the main inn of the region, a description followed by an oneiric vision portraying the ruined inn or *antro* ("cave"), its innkeeper, and other shadows living there. From the consistent, ordinary, and logical reality of the arrival in La Portada, the reader moves gradually into the dreamlike world of the cave where the characters stay. Its entrance, instead of a door, is a hole, and in its bar (says the narrator to rarefy this new reality further), along with shadows like men or vice versa, there are a few cases of beer, probably the same kind of beer that quelled Rossmithal's thirst, a few bottles of cheap brandy, the kind old adventurers drank to entertain themselves for the last time, before perishing in the hostile land of La Portada (15).

As part of the same narrative perspective for transforming reality, the narrator casually passes on to the reader a few pieces of information he has gathered concerning the innkeeper. Notice how they are presented, as if they were merely rumors, not as verifiable truths. "Some say that he is a dangerous sage who, after having eliminated almost half of the Slavonian population, found for himself a refuge in La Portada; others believe that he is simply an impostor; still others, that he is a common criminal who, working as a guide for an Italian gynecologist, killed him, took his money and came to live in Spain." As if all these rumors were not enough, the narrator adds another one, more colorful than the rest: that the innkeeper is a Ukrainian Bolshevik who keeps in the attic one of the Czar's nieces, a victim whom he kidnapped just before coming to La Portada (15–16). To disparate rumors as to his identity, some strange and bizarre reports concerning his present activities are added. Some say—and the narrator believes it is true—that the innkeeper's main occupation is personally to take care of his business. And how does he do it? Sleeping from dawn to dusk. Others have added that he never sleeps at night because he is busy desecrating tombs; furthermore, that back in the corral he has three or four vicious dogs that, although they never bark, are trained to bite any "approaching animal of warm blood" (16–17).

Obviously this accumulation of disparate and bizarre rumors produces a threefold effect: it injects humor into an otherwise dry, monotonous text; it makes of the character in question a legendary figure; and it consolidates the engimatic, oneiric, and absurd nature of the world in the cave. To walk in it is to enter a strange, desolate reality, different from the one formed by the characters' arrival on the bus. This particular device, of objective accumulation of rumors, is not, of course, new in the author's fiction. It was employed in his major earlier works, especially in *You Will Return to Región,* where the narrator collected all the rumors on Numa's identity, and in *A Winter Journey,* concerning the *Intruso.*

Other characters are treated with the same perspective; and the effects are similar. The sixty-year-old Hervás, who seems to be the chief organizer of the group's vacation, is "contradictorily" and absurdly "fat and skinny, wide and narrow, weak and vigorous."

He wears clothes that are loose and at the same time tight and short. And his personality also seems to fit these absurdities (14) and incongruous descriptions. He is basically a lonely man. No one listens to him because, just like many narrators in Benet's texts, he has the habit of dragging on unnecessary explanations that put anyone to sleep (13). Even his closest friends, Mrs. Somer and Ricardo, who at times think highly of him, believe and are in fact convinced that he is simply a pretentious, stupid, miserable, ignorant man, a mad-cap, a liar, a perfect fool (52). The humor quite evident here derives from Somer's and Ricardo's appraisal of Hervás, whom they admire and at the same time despise, and from the accumulation of insults that, more than hurting the intended victim, seem to revert to those who chose to insult him. Ricardo and Somer, in their own solitude, realize that, despite what they think or say about Hervás, he is their only hope and ultimate redeemer. And what is worse, Hervás is fully aware that they admire and despise him, and that they need him as their savior. The moment he is aware of them, he regards his help to Somer and Ricardo as part of a "providential mission" he must carry on (52). Furthermore, this providential mission gives "meaning" to his own existence. So the three must continue with their contradictions and the nonsensical situation of mutual dependency. They have no choice. Their mutual company is their isolation. Somer and Ricardo must listen to what Hervás has to say to them even though they do not understand a word he is saying. And Hervás must continue with his providential mission and with his eloquent speeches that no one comprehends or that simply make no sense (49–56).

Their trip and the cave where they are to stay operate as symbolic elements within the novel. They have abandoned the apartment on Almirante Street, in the city, to come to the cave *(antro)*, which is their subconscious, hoping to find their identity that on the other side (the city), with reason alone, they could not find. They seek self-discovery by way of their inner, subconscious world. The shadows they encounter in the cave are nothing but their own subconscious selves or alter egos. This confrontation or dialogue, between the outer and inner selves, the conscious and subconscious egos, between characters and shadows, as one must expect, does not lead anywhere and is of no help. Instead it plunges them into further confusion and despair, turning their trip to La Portada into another cruel evidence of man's failure and absurdity. This journey or trip image to portray man's hope and failure to find his identity, to explain his own being here and now, is not new to Benet's readers, for it appears in several of his main books of fiction, especially *You Will Never Get Anywhere, You Will Return to Región,* and *A Winter Journey.*

In the State offers a multiple narrative point of view, quite appropriate for unveiling the complex actions and interactions of the outer and inner selves of the characters. Most of the eighteen chapters are developed with a distinctive variant of narrative point of view; this causes the structure of the work to be uneven, intensely complex, and enigmatic, where continuity is minimal while fragmentation and dislocation are prevalent.

The first and most important variant in narrative point of view is the third-person narrator, who relates the story of the three vacationers; sometimes he appears omniscient and sometimes the opposite, as ignorant of the subject as the reader or the characters. But he never fails in one thing: in being verbose, just like any other character in the work. More than a coherent exposition of thoughts, facts, and situations, his vivid and detailed narration constitutes a massive, alienating discourse whose only effect is to confuse and lead the reader nowhere. In view of this, one may say that his narrative duties and performance reflect the three characters' mission in life, to talk and talk without really communicating anything at all or at least anything meaningful or that makes any sense. Somer and Ricardo do not understand all that Hervás has to say but they must listen to him just as he must talk to them, in a kind of mutual entertainment to kill time and partially overcome their solitude. Clearly, in *In the State* language is not a means to communicate a logical system of ideas, but an end in itself, a case of the value of the word for word's sake. The word is there to play with and thus kill the boredom of time and existence. The narrator says repeatedly with ironic undertones in the middle of the sinuous and tortuous course of his narration: "as the valiant reader will remember" or as "that patient reader will remember" (17, 171). Of course, the "patient" and "valiant" reader not only does not remember what the narrator expects to be remembered, but actually there is nothing to remember, except the confusion or nonsense undergone at certain points in the discourse. It is also humorous and ironic the way he calls his characters "our old friend Mr. Hervás" or "our hero" (17, 109), revealing that he is cognizant of the fact that Mr. Hervás is a fictional hero even though (from what the narrator said about Hervás earlier) the reader has a definite and opposite idea about the character in question: that he is an antihero. To secure the reliability of his narrative role and therefore the authenticity of this incredible story, the narrator resorts to a variety of casual devices typical of the realist novel of the nineteenth century. For instance, he settles the matter of the rumors concerning the innkeeper's daily activities by picking one of them as a verifiable truth and leaving the others as they are, merely rumors: "But what is certain is that the man restricts himself to managing his business for which it is enough for him to sleep permanently from dawn to dusk" (16). But this information is of almost no use, because it simply reveals another absurdity, the absurdity of a man managing his business by sleeping from dawn to dusk. To buttress the narrator's reliability, statements such as the following are used: "one has to tell everything, when one chooses a specific type of chronicle" (29), showing his full understanding of the nature, effects, and repercussions of one particular narrative method.

Besides the third-person description there are other narrative methods the general narrator employs to articulate his material:

Extensive Dialogues Moderated by the Third-Person Narrator. Most of the chapters in the book are built and developed through this method. These dialogues are normally carried on by mysterious characters, by the shadows inhabiting the inn, and by the shadows with one of the three vacationers. All " 'discussions are futile that lead nowhere' " (171); they are mere products of the tongue, which, like the pen of the author, "seems to run alone" with no apparent logical reason or control (188). Here the dialoguists, like the omniscient narrator himself, who allows their direct participation, gather minute details so flagrantly absurd and ridiculous that sometimes one must question the validity of the entire linguistic experiment unless one is to take such nonsensical verbiage as a paradigmatic embodiment of man's ontological futility (evident in Hervás, Somer, and Ricardo). Of special importance from this point of view are chapters XIII and XVI. But a more effective dialogue is found in chapter X, where Gemisto and Genadio (reminiscent of Vladimir and Estragon in *Waiting for Godot,* a work Benet considers a "literary monument built to the futility of human life"[44] cannot find a way out of their futile discussion, which is in itself a representation of futile existence. They are forever trapped by the nonsense of their own Hamletian dilemma of to be or not to be (113–22).

First-Person Interpolations. When neither dialogue nor third-person narration is employed, the general narrator allows characters or shadows to present their views and facts directly to the reader without intermediaries. With these interpolations the objectivity and the ironic and humorous tone of the text gain intensity since the character himself is the one who baits his own trap; the reader sees him alone, battling his obsessions, thoughts, and discourse. This device is used in chapters XI and XIV, where Mrs. Somer's subconscious self tells the story of how and when she lost her virginity, along with all the effects, consequences, and bitterness caused by her bizarre, premature sexual experience. As her confession unfolds, the ludicrousness of the episode, circumstances, and consequences are clarified so that the reader's reaction changes from sympathy to pure laughter. In chapters VIII and XII, the colonel painstakingly and meticulously presents his intricate plan of war to Mrs. Somer without realizing that he is merely boring her and the reader. And the more he talks the more he alienates himself from his listeners. The main narrator cannot deter him since he has given the character freedom. As the master of his own destiny and discourse, the character, not the narrator, must be accountable for what he does and says, for his own absurdity, even though unaware of that absurdity, resulting from his actions and words, which the "patient" and "valiant" reader or listener must tolerate.

As in his other fictional works, in *In the State* Benet equates time with emptiness and futility, an equation which leads in turn to perceiving the present as being as empty as the past and the future as empty as the present—it is the vision of a never-ending concatenation of temporal steps devoid of all human significance. "Time is not complete and neither is matter, and within it there are vacuums which are closed and isolated from each other like bubbles in liquids." That is why, says one character to another, "I ask you, between yesterday and today how much nothingness has taken place? For how long have we been dead . . . ? And when we awake, are we the same person or a different one, endowed with the schemeful power of memory . . . that makes one person believe that he continues to be the same one in order to abolish the hope threaded by death?" (150). Since the character anticipates impotence and futility in the future because the past offered him exactly that, the present becomes an ongoing verification of that future (185), a self-fulfilling prophecy. This philosophical dilemma has some bearing on the actual manipulation of time in the novel. Novelistic or narrative time in *In the State* does not vary significantly from the manner in which it is handled in Benet's earlier works. Yet a few key cases require analysis since they generate special effects in the work's narrative process. Using the command and the present tense, the third-person narrator instructs the reader: "look how he (Mr. Hervás, who has just gotten off the bus) dusts his trousers and lapels of his jacket, how he fixes the knot of his tie and how, holding the cuff of his shirt with two fingers, brushes his black hat with his forearm . . ." (17). The use of the command "look" definitely affects the reading of the passage, inviting the reader to visualize all the specific moves (or actions expressed through the present tense) of the character. The natural sequence and casual manner in which they are executed enhance the visual impact of the scene. Under similar circumstances, most people would likely do what Hervás did.

The special use of the future appears in chapter XII, while its effects are articulated in the past in chapter XVII. One without the other cannot be understood. In chapter XII the colonel presents to Mrs. Somer all the military moves and tactics they *will* follow in order to win the forthcoming war; the use of the future tense obviously prevails here. In chapter XVII, the same colonel asks Mrs. Somer, now that the war has already taken place, how she liked the tactical moves outlined in chapter XII and thereafter followed with precision in the war. He repeats those moves but now using the past since they have already been executed. "Did you see the attack of the 37th Division? . . . Marvelous, right?" (197, 197–205). Here, there has been an actual transformation of novelistic time: the future has become the past, yet has brought nothing save the perpetuation of futility evident in the linguistic emptiness achieved through the strategic nonsense transmitted by the colonel to Mrs. Somer within the future tense in chapter XII and with the past in chapter XVII. In Benet's works, philosophical time is compatible with narrative time. The former sets the pattern for the latter. What the characters perceive of the first is embodied in the second, which in turn is ultimately the force determining the actual structure of the work and its narrative process.

Certain special stylistic devices of ironic or parodic effects worthy of note in the novel are: the grotesque, linguistic accumulations and repetitions, onomastic proliferations, and allusion to other literary texts.

The Grotesque. It is used purposely and with great intensity, to reinforce the overall atmosphere of absurdity and the oneiric side of many episodes whose main unifying force is precisely the grotesque perspective with which they are conceived and developed. A key example of this is the premature and abrupt defloration of the future Mrs. Somer by her senile uncle on the very same day she received her first communion, an incident she will never forget because of both the traumatic effects on her personality and the nagging physical pain she always feels in the respective area of her body (70–77). She becomes an active initiate in religion and sex at the same time. The grotesqueness of it all is heightened by the form of narration. She is the narrator of her own story, but without her realizing it the account moves in such a way as to emphasize quite dramatically the fact that she became an active participant in religion and sex at the same time; that her double initiation was achieved via two incongruous symbols, semen and Eucharist (37–46): and that, afterwards, she must undergo spiritual and physical pain. The incident, her obsession, becomes an obsession in the novel, an articulate, forceful, and recurrent symbol. The author's aim with the incident seems to have been to parody the severe Spanish-Catholic morality ruling sex, family, and religion, perverted and distorted through Mrs. Somer, who in the book is handled as an archetypal symbol of the Spanish woman.

Accumulation and Repetition. In every chapter or narrative unit, the narrator is fascinated or obsessed by the need to overwhelm his presentation with a massive accumulation of information, making it impossible for the reader to assimilate a logical idea of events. Massiveness suffocates content, and stifles continuity in the discourse's line of thought. Chapters XII, XVI, or XVII, for instance, are artistically successful units not because of their content—in fact they "mean" nothing—but because of their linguistic construction. They constitute amorphous accumulations of details concerning tactics of war and data on books; the "pleasure" of reading comes from the sound of language and its mere presence on the page, not from what it actually says or communicates. The act of writing, it seems, is justified by the form, not its content—form being here equivalent to style. Benet's technique of accumulation is aptly synthesized by the colonel to Mrs. Somer when urged to explain his military plans: "I will not overwhelm you with technical details or with data that can only be of interest to the specialist, yet given the fact that we have here a plan extraordinarily complex and studied with extreme care, unknown to this day, I will go into details covering matters that in principle you will regard as secondary, but that will help you very much to understand the whole" (96). In a way his subsequent explanation is a microcosmic representation of the novel itself. Repetition of words or statements produce similar effects: laughter, a sense of futility, total nonsense. Somer asks Hervás: "Have we arrived [in La Portada]? He replies: "Yes, we have arrived . . . we have arrived well. It is not a small thing; it has not been easy; no way has it been easy; no way. Definitely it has not been easy. No way. But we have arrived" (19). Boasting of her family's possessions, Mrs. Somer, enthusiastic, articulates the following statement: "They had lands with thousands of trees, thousands and thousands of trees, thousands of bushels, dozens of thousands, hundreds of thousands, thousands of thousands of hundreds of thousands, millions of bushels, of acres . . ." (37–38). Her pride and ambition are ridiculed through excessive repetition, the ironic embodiment of her excessive wealth.

Onomastic Proliferation. More than any other of Benet's works, *In the State* provides a veritable mine of names of real or imaginary people and places, an onomastic orgy. Complex spelling and pronunciation generate mystery, laughter, and, conversely, an apparent sense of objectivity and accuracy of description on the part of the narrator (chapters XII, XVI, XVII).

Allusions to Other Texts. One cannot miss Benet's deliberate stylistic allusions to other works either to parody or to pay tribute to their authors while also enriching, with stylistic variety, his own text. Obviously, chapter X is a tribute to Samuel Beckett. From every point of view, be this technical or philosophical, Gemisto's dialogue with Genadio is reminiscent of the lonely and futile conversation held by Estragon with Vladimir or Lucky with Pozzo in *Waiting for Godot.* In the same chapter, one of the dialoguists, reflecting on the grave dilemma of man (to be or not to be), says, elaborating upon the thoughts of Segismundo in the most eloquent soliloquy of *Life Is a Dream:*

"Due entirely to this indeterminality to be is not to be,
that which cannot be named"
that is despair
is honor
is fate
is courage
is frenzy
is fury, is anger
and finally, is there nothing to satiate your blind passion? (119)

Describing Ricardo's youthful years, a parody of Rubén Darío and his *modernistas* followers is evident.[45] He, Ricardo, has been in touch with "a new generation of artists and poets in whose enigmatic verses, sometimes, appeared Parténope and Azur" (*Azul* is one of Darío's most important works) (32). As previously noted, the Generation of 1898 (especially Azorín, with his emotive and detailed description of Castille) also becomes the victim of Benet's parody when portraying La Portada as an austere and desolate land for contemplation, meditation, and, incidentally, brutalization.

Chapter Eight
Conclusion

At the end of this exploratory journey through the life and works of Juan Benet a few concluding reflections will clarify and reiterate key ideas concerning his fabulous world of fiction and his unique place in the contemporary Spanish novel. Benet, one of the top new novelists in the Spanish language, must be placed among other contemporary novelists such as Vargas Llosa, Carlos Fuentes, García Márques, or Juan Goytisolo (of the last three novels). In the last decade he has become one of the most controversial and influential men in Spain today. His influence as a novelist and as a thinker is strongly felt among young writers, especially in Barcelona. And with his work steadily growing each year, his influence will logically become greater.

Benet's fictional world is unique, complex, mysterious, demanding, enigmatic, and aesthetically rewarding. To enter the world of Región is to enter a labyrinth where everything—except ruin, death and futility—is uncertain, or a tantalizing approximation. Solutions or answers to problems or questions are never given, and perceptions are often blurred by unreliable narrators who are sure neither of themselves nor of that which they relate, even recounting realities which never existed. Deliberately, Benet undermines the basic reliability of his narrator, as part of his ironic vision of man caught in a world where nothing is absolute and everything is relative. Olympian omniscience crumbles with the narrator caught in his own intricacies, contradictions, fears, and confusions; other spectral creatures in the narration also fall into the concealed traps of ambition, self-confidence, and passion leading them to solitude, ruin, and death. And they can neither stop nor change the course of predetermined ruination because time is the confirmation of failures and not of regeneration. Their existential apothegm is, "I suffer therefore I am." Efforts are futile. The more they talk and strive to explain reality, the more elusive it becomes; like Benet's marathon sentences, the more his prose runs uninterrupted the more elusive its content becomes.

This linguistic intensity is another exteriorization of the intensity of the character's inner, tragic conflict between a desire to know more about himself and the world and the inefficacy of his linguistic means or his inherent ontological limitation. Seeking the causes for their on-going failure, his characters find not a satisfactory answer but an elusive, mysterious "truth": that the present failure is the result of a past failure whose causes cannot be explained satisfactorily. And they are inexplicable because memory cannot recall all necessary elements in order to create a satisfactory picture of past failures. Instinctively they seek "truth," but reason and memory deny them that pleasure. Irony and absurdity, again, are omnipresent in Benet's fictional world: characters strive for something and end up with quite the opposite as if invisible, malignant forces of absurdity were guiding them to failure and nothingness. And neither the victim (the character), the narrator, nor the reader understands why, how, where, or when failure began to take possession of man.

Benet, as said earlier, does not work with certainties. His world is built with ambiguities or enigmas which permeate the entire novelistic fabric. Plot does not exist, or if it does it is kept to a minimum, merely a pretext to satiate the author's capricious imagination. Any mobility in the novel is perceived mainly through recurrent images that become more and more complex upon each recurrence. Since past, present, and future are only symbols of emptiness or nothingness, meaningful chronological sequence of events does not exist. Characters are not developed according to traditional tenets of depiction. They are, for the most part, shadows or specters in permanent struggle with themselves, their futility, and their ruin. More than dynamic, changing entities, they are immobile figures unable to find their way. The structures of the works are labyrinthine, resembling never-ending puzzles, intricate mosaics of opaque mirrors, prisms of reality tinted with illusion, dreams redreamed and vaguely remembered by a lonely, nostalgic consciousness.

Notes and References

Chapter One

1. Juan Benet, "De Canudos a Macondo," *Revista de Occidente*, 2ª Epoca, 24, no. 70 (January 1969):50–51. His mentors' evaluation is utterly unfounded and ridiculous. And even the authors themselves would admit it. A great deal of information on Benet's life has been extracted from Barbara Probst Solomon, *Los felices cuarenta (Una educación sentimental)* (Barcelona: Editorial Seix Barral, S.A., 1978). This is a translation from the original: *Arriving Where We Started* (New York: Harper and Row Publishers, Inc., 1972). Because of the special circumstances in which I wrote this chapter, I was forced to use the Spanish translation, the only one available to me.

2. Benet, "De Canudos," p. 52.

3. Ibid. ,

4. See Juan Benet, "Barojiana" in *Barojiana,* a special collection of essays written by several contemporary writers on Pío Baroja's personality and works (Madrid: Taurus Ediciones, S.A., 1972), p. 12.

5. Probst Solomon, *Los felices,* pp. 241–42.

6. Juan Benet, "Breve historia de *Volverás a Región,"* *Revista de Occidente,* 2ª Epoca, 45, no. 134 (May 1974):160–61.

7. Antonio Núñez, "Encuentro con Juan Benet," *Insula* 24, no. 269 (April 1969):4.

Chapter Two

1. Gonzalo Sobejano, "Direcciones de la novela española de postguerra" in *Novelistas Españoles de Postguerra,* Edición de Rodolfo Cardona, El Escritor y la Crítica (Madrid: Taurus Ediciones, S.A., 1976), p. 47. It was originally published in *Boletín de la Asociación Europea de Profesores de Español* 4 (6 March 1972):55–73.

2. Sobejano, "Direcciones," pp. 49–50.

3. For a good study of irony in this novel, see Mary Ann Beck, "Nuevo encuentro con la *Familia de Pascual Duarte,"* in Cardona, *Novelistas,* pp. 65–88.

4. Taken from José María Martínez Cachero, *Historia de la novela española entre 1936 y 1975* (Madrid: Editorial Castalia, 1979), p. 73.

5. Ibid.

6. Ibid., p. 71.

7. This statement by Cela has been taken from Manuel Alvar, "Noventa y ocho y novela de postguerra," in Cardona, *Novelistas,* p. 35.

8. Pablo Gil Casado, *La novela social española,* 2ª edición (Barcelona: Editorial Seix Barral, S.A., 1975), p. 121.

9. It is the word with which the new movement came to be identified.

10. Martínez Cachero, *Historia,* p. 236.

11. Ibid., p. 228.

12. Benet, "Respuesta al Señor Montero," *Cuadernos para el Diálogo* 23 (December 1970):75.

13. Martínez Cachero, *Historia,* pp. 160–61.

14. Benet, "Reflexiones sobre Galdós," *Cuadernos para el Diálogo* 23 (December 1970):13–15.

15. Isaac Montero, "Acotación a una mesa redonda (Respuestas a Juan Benet y defensa apresurada del realismo)," *Cuadernos para el Diálogo* 23 (December 1970):65–74.

16. Benet, "Reflexiones," p. 13.

17. Benet, "Respuesta al Señor Montero," p. 76.

Chapter Three

1. Because of the politicohistoric nature of its content, *What Was the Civil War?* is not studied in this book. For textual references I put the title of the books and the page number in parentheses, but this is done only in this chapter. In the other chapters the page number alone in parentheses is used. With the exception of *Inspiration and Style* I use the first edition of all Benet's books of essays; in this one instance, the second one is used, as appears in the Bibliography.

2. For his discussions Benet often resorts to a comparative method of concepts, contrasting the nature of one in relation to another, thus shaping the analysis of both. For this matter see also David Herzberger, *The Novelistic World of Juan Benet* (Clear Creek, Ind., 1976), pp. 21–41.

3. Benet, *En ciernes* (Madrid, 1976), pp. 84–102.

Chapter Four

1. Benet, *Teatro* (Madrid, 1971). I exclude *Max* (1953) because the author himself has never regarded it as part of his formal literary output. A brief but good review of this book can be found in Raúl Moncada Galán, "Juan Benet," *El Día* 85 (15 June 1974):ix.

2. From the letter to me by the author dated 6 August 1979.

3. Moncada Galán says, "To us *Agonia Confutans* seems to be more a philosophical essay than a genuine theatrical work" ("Juan Benet," p. ix).

Chapter Five

1. Antonio Núñez, "Encuentro con Juan Benet," *Insula* 24, no. 269 (April 1969):4. Here I used this second edition, as appears in the Bibliography.

2. José Domingo, "Eduardo Tijeras, G. Torrente Malvido, Juan Benet," *Insula* 25, no. 278 (January 1970):5.

3. Benet states repeatedly that what interests him the most is not the character but "the enigma of the character, his drama and not the street." See this in Danubio Torres Fierro, "Juan Benet: La literatura no es sicología; el enigma da la profundidad," *Excelsior,* 12 May 1974, p. 3.

4. See Ricardo Gullón, "Sobre espectros y tumbas," *Cuaderno de Norte: Revista Hispánica de Amsterdam,* 1976, p. 83–95; Herzberger, *Novelistic World of Juan Benet,* pp. 101–14. I use the first edition of this work, as appears in the Bibliography.

5. Gullón, "Sobre espectros," p. 83.

6. Herzberger, *Novelistic World,* p. 109.

7. We do not know who the lady, or *señora,* really is. It seems, however, that she was a lover of the child's uncle, his father's brother.

8. The cold, casual description gives the impression that the horror of its content is natural in the relations between the assailants and the victims within this novelistic context.

9. Herzberger, *Novelistic World,* pp. 106–7.

10. All quotations are from the first edition of *Sub Rosa* (Barcelona, 1973).

11. He was convicted for having caused the sinking of the boat.

12. Ricardo Gullón, *"Sub Rosa"* (Review), *Journal of Spanish Studies: Twentieth Century* 3, no. 2 (Fall 1975):145.

13. References are to the first edition of *Del Pozo y del Numa (un ensayo y una leyenda)* (Barcelona, 1978).

14. So the novelette, which at the beginning seemed to be a process of definition, in the end proves to be only a tantalizing approximation, for Numa remains what we already knew he was: an enigma.

Chapter Six

1. Benet, "Prólogo," in *Cuentos Completos* (Madrid: Alianza Editorial, 1977), 1:8–9.

2. All quotations and references are to the first edition of *5 narraciones y dos fábulas* (Barcelona, 1972).

3. Walter de la Mare (1873–1956) was an English novelist, short-story writer, and poet. Among his many works are *Memoirs of a Midget, Peacock Pie,* and *The Listeners.*

4. See *The Ghost Stories of Edith Wharton* (New York: Charles Scribner's Sons, 1973), p. 4.

5. The professor in "Syllabus" is the only character with a name.
6. The two fables are not included in his *Cuentos Completos.*
7. The division into parts one and two is used to facilitate the study of the story.
8. Sergio Gómez Parra, "Juan Benet: la ruptura de un horizonte novelístico," *Reseña* 9 (1972):3–12.
9. This novelette was studied in Chapter 5. All references and quotations are to the first edition of *Sub Rosa* (Barcelona, 1973).
10. Janet Díaz, "Death in the Short Stories of Juan Benet," unpublished paper delivered at a special session on Juan Benet in the MLA Convention of 1977.
11. C. Durán used to be the number-one man of the group.
12. It is as if she felt compelled to fill with her nephew the vacuum left by her husband and sons.
13. The people he wants to help are those sitting at the table.
14. It is as though he had tape-recorded almost the entire story told by the second narrator.
15. Janet Díaz, "Death."
16. Honorio, says Benet, "symbolizes the virtues of the race and of Franco's victory." Torres Fierro, "Juan Benet," p. 3.
17. He ran into Baretto accidentally and not purposely. At least this is what Gavilanes says. He may or may not be telling the truth. One will never know.

Chapter Seven

1. Cited in Miguel Fernández Braso, *De escritor a escritor* (Barcelona: Editorial Taber, 1970), p. 198.
2. Benet, "Breve historia de *Volverás a Región,*" *Revista de Occidente,* 2ª Epoca, 45, no. 134 (May 1974):160–65. Among the many good studies on this novel, the following are of special interest and value: Herzberger, *Novelistic World,* pp. 43–69; Ricardo Gullón, "Una región laberíntica que bien pudiera llamarse España," *Insula* 29, no. 319 (June 1973):3, 10; Manual Durán, "Juan Benet y la nueva novela española," *Cuadernos Americanos* 33, no. 4 (July-August 1974):193–205. For other studies on the subject see Malcolm Alan Compitello's useful "Bibliography: Juan Benet and His Critics," *Anales de la Novela de Postguerra* 3 (1978):123–41.
3. The edition used here is Benet, *Volverás a Región* (Barcelona, 1967).
4. Durán, "Juan Benet," p. 202.
5. Benet says, concerning the basic structure of this novel, that "it rests on a tripod (like Christ's church), three perfectly heterogeneous feet; they are: the myth of the Guard [Numa] and of the sacred forest, the development and consequences of the Civil War . . . and the disorders

caused by a frustrated, pseudomarriage in the middle of the mountain" (*Volverás*, p. 162).

6. E. M. Forster, *Aspects of the Novel* (New York: Harcourt, Brace & World, 1927), p. 96.

7. The statement reminds one of Mr. Compson's statement, in *The Sound and the Fury*, that man "is the sum of his misfortunes."

8. See Alberto Oliart, "Viaje a Región," *Revista de Occidente* 27, no. 80 (November 1969):229.

9. Pere Gimferrer adds: "it may be one of the peaks in the Spanish narrative of this century." See this in his *Radicalidades* (Barcelona, 1978), p. 131. The edition used here is *Una meditación* (Barcelona: Editorial Seix Barral, 1970).

10. Núñez, "Encuentro," p. 4.

11. Herzberger, *Novelistic World,* p. 98.

12. Often Benet's comments on his own works are deliberately misleading.

13. The concept of "memory's fallibility" is essential to the understanding of this and many other works of Benet.

14. See Herzberger's comments on the subject: *Novelistic World,* pp. 74–80.

15. Similar effects are perceived in Juan Goytisolo's *Juan sin Tierra,* Cabrera Infante's *Tres tristes tigres,* and of course in *Don Quijote.*

16. It is precisely what he does in his *A la Recherche du temps perdu.*

17. Similar formulation of time appeared originally in *You Will Return to Región* and will reappear throughout his later works, especially in *A Winter Journey* and *In the State.*

18. Says Herzberger in *Novelistic World,* p. 88:

Through his sexual gratification, claims Freud, man becomes a higher being, committed to higher values than the primordial urges associated with pure instincts. The sexuality of man is dignified by love—i.e., sexuality with affection. In *Una meditación,* however, Benet debases the Freudian theory of love and sexuality by frequently reducing the characters to their animalistic, instinctual drives. Benet achieves this effect in two significant ways: 1) by the creation of similes and metaphors in which human beings are compared to animals; 2) by using Freudian related sex symbols, through which the characters' sex drives are related to animalistic imagery.

19. This *desesperanza* permeates the entire narrative discourse, becoming an obsession, similar to his endeavor to recover the past and understand it.

20. The definition is taken from Philip Thompson, *The Grotesque* (London: Methuen Co., 1972), p. 2.

21. For further discussion of this symbol see José Ortega, *Ensayos de la novela española moderna* (Madrid: Ediciones José Porrúa Turanzas, S.A., 1974), p. 162, and also Herzberger, *Novelistic World,* pp. 89–90.

22. These are the adjectives used by critics to identify Benet's typical, long, sinuous sentence.

23. Thus Benet's text becomes literary creation as well as literary criticism.

24. All quotations are from the first edition of *Un viaje de invierno* (Barcelona: La Gaya Ciencia, 1972).

25. See Ortega, *Ensayos,* p. 165.

26. I will study this idea in detail when I analyze the recurrent images in the novel.

27. These marginal notes are studied later with the narrative point of view.

28. References to the nostalgic consciousness are found on pages 21, 31, 78, 172–73, 176, 178, 201, 222, 227, 238, 239.

29. Ricardo Gullón, "Esperando a Coré," *Revista de Occidente,* 2ª Epoca, 49, no. 143 (April 1975):16–20.

30. Ibid., p. 19.

31. Sharon Spencer, concerning mobile constructs, says that "the poetics of space in the novel is based upon the assumption that, in our time, to perceive, comprehend, or apprehend any object, the perceptor must accumulate a variety of perspectives upon that object. He must 'see' from as many points of view as possible" (*Space, Time and Structure in the Modern Novel* [Chicago: The Swallow Press, 1971], pp. 185–86).

32. Herzberger, *Novelistic World,* p. 116.

33. Just as in his other novels.

34. Gonzalo Sobejano, *Novela española de nuestro tiempo (en busca del pueblo perdido),* 2ª edición (Madrid, 1975), pp. 580–81. See also Ortega, *Ensayos,* p. 166.

35. Herzberger facilitates the study of the *bausán,* the horse, and the crows by offering perceptive comments and also by giving a useful list of all the pages where these symbols appear. See *Novelistic World,* pp. 125, 131, 135. See also Gullón's interpretations of these symbols: "Esperando," pp. 32–35.

36. See Antonio Machado, *Poesías completas,* duodécima edición (Madrid: Espasa-Calpe, 1969), pp. 52–53.

37. Other references to the helpless musician are found on pages 67, 141, 155, 204, 233, 236, 240–41.

38. For other textual references to the intruder see pages 49, 109, 115, 191.

39. It is distinguished from the rest of the novel by appearing on yellow paper. My colleague Klaus Hoffman helped me in this translation from the German.

40. This was studied when I discussed Arturo and Demetria's relationship, and the nostalgic consciousness.

41. See Herzberger, *Novelistic World,* p. 135.

42. Cited in Torres Fierro, "Juan Benet," p. 3. Similarities between Benet's *The Mazóns' Other House* and Faulkner's *Requiem for a Nun* are obvious, not only because of the use of narrative and dramatic forms but also because of the affinities encountered in plot episodes and thematic treatments. This is largely inconsequential, however, because Benet's work constitutes a singular expression of a unique and original perception. See Herzberger, *Novelistic World,* pp. 137, 142–43, 152. See also Darío Villanueva, "Las narraciones de Juan Benet," in *Novela española actual,* ed. Andrés Amorós (Madrid, 1977), pp. 166–69. The edition I use of this novel is *La otra casa de Mazón* (Barcelona, 1973).

43. I use the first edition of *En el estado* (Madrid, 1977). An excellent review of this novel is found in David Herzberger, *"En el estado," Anales de la Novela de Posguerra* 3 (1978):143–44.

44. Benet, "Samuel Beckett, Premio Nobel, 1969." *Revista de Occidente,* 2ª Epoca, 28, no. 83 (February 1970):229.

45. This is another case of parody and of literary creation through literary criticism.

Selected Bibliography

PRIMARY SOURCES

El ángel del señor abandona a Tobías. Barcelona: La Gaya Ciencia, 1976.
5 narraciones y 2 fabulas. Barcelona: La Gaya Ciencia, 1972.
Del pozo y del Numa. Barcelona: La Gaya Ciencia, 1978.
En ciernes. Madrid: Taurus, 1976.
En el estado. Madrid: Alfaguara, 1977.
La inspiración y el estilo. Madrid: Revista de Occidente, 1965. 2a ed.
   Barcelona: Seix Barral, 1974.
Una meditación. Barcelona: Seix Barral, 1970.
Nunca llegarás a nada. Madrid: Editorial Tebas, 1961. 2a ed. Madrid:
   Alianza Editorial, 1969.
La otra casa de Mazón. Barcelona: Seix Barral, 1973.
¿Qué fué la guerra civil? Barcelona: La Gaya Ciencia, 1976.
Sub rosa. Barcelona: La Gaya Ciencia, 1973.
Teatro. Madrid: Siglo XXI de España, 1971.
Una tumba. Barcelona: Lumen, 1971.
Volverás a Región. Barcelona: Destino, 1967; 2a ed. Madrid: Alianza Ed-
   itorial, 1974.

SECONDARY SOURCES

1. Book

Herzberger, David K. *The Novelistic World of Juan Benet.* Clear Creek,
   Ind.: The American Hispanist, 1977. The first and most comprehensive study of Benet's major novels and literary theory.

2. Articles

Aveleyra A., Teresa. "Algo sobre las criaturas de Juan Benet." *Nueva
   Revista de Filología Hispánica* 23, no. 1 (1974): 121–30. Using *You
   Will Return to Región* and *A Meditation,* the author finds fear as the
   main force in the characters' ruined world and strange, surreal behavior.

Carrasquer, Francisco. "*Cien años de soledad* y *Volverás a Región,* dos polos." *Norte: Revista Hispánica de Amsterdam* 11, no. 6 (November–December 1970):197–201. An interesting relationship between two important fictional worlds in twentieth-century Hispanic literature.

Durán, Manuel. "Juan Benet y la nueva novela española." *Cuadernos Americanos* 195, no. 4 (July–August 1974):193–205. An appraisal of Benet's role in the contemporary Spanish novel. Durán views Benet— along with Torrente Ballester, Juan Goytisolo, Martín Santos, Cela, and others—as the new alternative for the Spanish novel.

Gimferrer, Pere. "Notas sobre Juan Benet." In *Radicalidades.* Barcelona: Bosch, Casa Editorial, 1978, pp. 125–38. An overview of Benet's major novels by one of his closest friends and admirers.

Guillermo, Edenia, and Hernández, Juana Amelia. "Juan Benet. *Volverás a Región.* "In Edenia Guillermo and Juana Amelia Hernández, eds. *Novelística española de los sesenta.* New York: Eliseo Torres, 1971, pp. 130–50. One of the first studies of *You Will Return to Región.* It underscores its enigmatic and nonsensical nature. Chance, not will, determines the course of collective events and individual behavior.

Gullón, Ricardo. "Una región laberíntica que bien pudiera llamarse España." *Insula* 29, no. 319 (June 1973):2, 10. A brief yet fundamental analysis of *You Will Return to Región*'s time, space, and characters as well as its general ambiguity and surreal invention.

———. "Esperando a Coré." *Revista de Occidente* 49, no. 145 (April 1975):16–36. An excellent analysis of space, time, and symbols in *A Winter Journey.*

———. "Sobre espectros y tumbas." *Cuaderno de Norte: Revista Hispánica de Amsterdam.* Special issue on Augusto Roa Bastos and Juan Benet, 1976, pp. 83–95. An insightful study of *A Tomb* as a ghost story. In view of its artistic effects, the novelette is compared to stories such as *The Jolly Corner* or *A Small Boy and Others* by Henry James.

Herzberger, David K. "The Emergence of Juan Benet. A New Alternative for the Spanish Novel." *American Hispanist* 1, no. 3 (November 1975):6–12. Most of its content reappeared in his book, previously listed.

Marco, Joaquín. "Las obras recientes de Juan Benet." In Joaquín Marco, ed. *Nueva literatura en España y América.* Barcelona: Lumen, 1972, pp. 143–55. After a brief yet effective defense of Galdos's art, severely attacked by Benet, Marco unconvincingly explains the stylistic deficiencies of *A Meditation.* Later he makes generalizations on the novelistic merits of *A Tomb.*

Oliart, Alberto. "Viaje a Región." *Revista de Occidente,* 2ª Epoca, 27, no. 80 (November 1969):224–34. A review-article of *You Will Return to*

Región. It is perhaps the first attempt to reveal many of the thematic and stylistic traits that would typify Benet's subsequent fiction.

Ortega, José. "Estudios sobre la obra de Juan Benet." *Cuadernos Hispanoamericanos,* no. 284 (February 1974), pp. 229–58. A generally good study of Benet's so-called trilogy.

Sobejano, Gonzalo. "La novela estructural: de Luis Martín-Santos a Juan Benet." In Gonzalo Sobejano, ed., *Novela española de nuestro tiempo: en busca del pueblo perdido.* 2ª ed. Madrid: Prensa Española, 1975, pp. 545–609. The structural novel gains momentum, according to Sobejano, with Juan Benet's fictional world. And of special importance in this respect is the novelist's trilogy, to which the critic devotes insightful analysis.

Villanueva, Darío. "Las narraciones de Juan Benet." In Andrés Amorós, ed. *Novela española actual.* Madrid: Fundación Juan March/Ediciones Cátedra, 1977, pp. 133–72. A lengthy and well-documented monograph dealing with Benet's novelistic development. It also establishes interesting relations between the author and other major European and North American novelists such as Melville, Proust, Kafka, V. Woolf, Faulkner, etc.

3. Bibliographic Compilation

Compitello, Malcolm Alan. "Bibliography, Juan Benet and His Critics." *Anales de la Novela de Posguerra.* Vol. 3 (1978). A very useful tool for research on Juan Benet's literary creation, containing works by Benet and all previously published critical material written on him. Its accuracy and completeness make this bibliography indispensable.

Index